Hacking Fatherhood

Preparing for Success in the Biggest Role of your Life

by: Dr. Nate Dallas

D1114686

www.HackingFatherhoodBook.com

For orders or inquiries, please use the form on the website.

Copyright © 2016 Nathan J Dallas

Dedication

To my wife: You are my rock, my motivation, and my hero.
To my dad: Thank you for your living example of dedication,
manhood, and vocation.
To my four boys that I have the privilege of raising:
I am proud of you. I love you.
To my two children lost: Thank you for preparing
my heart to love more deeply.
I hope to meet you all in paradise.

Table of Contents

There's No Time Like the Present

Many of your friends may begin to dislike you, especially ones in the same stage in life. As they observe you becoming a successful father and husband, you will indirectly highlight their deficiencies, sometimes publicly. A dedicated man who shows wisdom, discipline, and leadership makes his household secure, but can simultaneously irritate peers. The insecure and guilty ones, which are many, may resent you for it. The world loves the indifferent and the ordinary but hates two classes of people: those who are too good, and those who are too bad. Everyone loves the underdog until he starts consistently winning. That underdog was a member of the normal, mediocre crowd before, but no longer. Now he has become an outlier and an unintentional whistleblower.

The title *Hacking Fatherhood* likely implies multiple meanings to different people based on interpretations and life experiences. Just to clear the air, I want to clarify my intent with the title. I do not mean to hack away at this, leaving a chopped up mess as a final product. In other words, I do not want to imply that anyone is a hack-job, just managing to scrape by with trial and error. The ready, fire, aim approach will produce a guaranteed failure in this area of grave importance. The verb that I want you to instill in your mind is the one popularly used in the areas of life hacking or computer hacking. This form of hacking means to win by beating the system, or at least by gaming the system in a more intelligent, lesser-known way. Hacking requires gaining knowledge that few others possess and finding creative and systematic ways to use that knowledge to a sizable advantage. You may associate this type of hacking with cheating. That's fine too. I feel like I am sometimes cheating, and that I am getting away with something when I compare my life to the ones around me. There is certainly nothing dishonest about it, it just feels like it's unfair to the world that I am able to beat the normal system by using knowledge and effort that is not readily available to the general public. I did not earn the right to be made privy to this classified information, and I find it disheartening that so few men are given the same package of information, parental modeling, and experience. That is exactly why this book now exists. To him whom much is given, much is expected, right?

Businesses fail. Friendships fail. Marriages fail. Why? The supermajority of these failures can be attributed to two simple concepts that are woefully complex: inaccurate expectations and poor preparation. I'm guessing that at this stage in your life, family failure is not an option. If that's true, then you are in the right place. It's time to discover realistic expectations and cultivate a superior plan for success.

I'm not sure how you wound up in this position of discerning fatherhood. On second thought, I have a decent idea. Some of you are here out of necessity and are late to the planning game. A sense of panic has set in because you know that a baby that shares your DNA is already on the way. The rest of you are way ahead of the typical process and are cautiously planning for a child to come along in the future. In either case, you are likely here because of love, even if you think you had a mishap or oversight. Love is a wonderful reason to be here, and the very foundation of how we will build this model. You may also be here because of passion. Love and passion have multiple meanings, and I'm sure that we can apply multiple definitions and situations to both terms in your story. Your emotions at this moment could include those of fear, panic, despair, diligence, dedication, pride, paranoia, resentment, negligence, satisfaction, excitement, or likely a combination of many. No one arrives at this stage of life in the same way, or at the same level of maturity, but the challenges that lie ahead are the same for all of us. That is, whether or not we can deny ourselves, make sacrifices, and commit to something bigger. Love is the gift of one's self. Loving is a conscious and deliberate choice.

This book is for the type of men who prefer working harder in order to get the job done more effectively. It's for guys who take pride in developing and expanding their skill set, and perhaps their own character—even if it requires more demanding labor—the dedication will be worth it in the end. It's for the self-motivated guy that isn't worried that he may distance himself from the safe and familiar crowd. In this book, we will eliminate distractions and plunge right into intense productivity. The effort will pay dividends in a rare currency also known as satisfaction. To be satisfied with our life's work, we need to use our time, talents, and effort for something important. So many people are dissatisfied in life because they know that they are wasting these things. Satisfaction comes from a union of body and soul. We must remain usefully engaged and challenged. It's about personal growth and true dedication to something of value. Nothing that we will ever do has the potential to benefit our lives as much as crushing this fatherhood role.

Satisfaction in this will beget peace and happiness that can only thrive in the absence of guilt. The rewards will be substantial, but not without setting lofty expectations, and accepting the need for personal sacrifice and commitment.

The tactical steps in this book will be built upon, time and time again. Success is cumulative and exponential. It never happens by accident. Starting well is the key, and discipline is everything. Reading this book and executing its strategies will prepare you to become proficient and enable you to be a true hacker. Just know that you may be resented for it—not praised or congratulated. You are probably optimistic and excited about being a father, but the fun-filled toddler and adolescent stages that we typically fantasize about come much later. Any legitimate chance for long-term success will depend on diligently and intentionally laying the proper groundwork now. Having smart, well-behaved, respectful, fun, loving children doesn't happen automatically. The hard truth is that if we have a child that doesn't respect authority, won't eat his vegetables, won't mind, can't do his chores, can't share, and cusses like a sailor—it's our fault. No one wants to admit it when it happens, but the foundation was certainly broken or maybe never laid in the first place. It's really hard to reel it back in if things get out of hand. The best defense here is a good offense.

There are many other manuals for expecting dads out there. Undoubtedly, many of them are pumped full of buzz words and statistics. The other books likely appeal to a broader audience looking for quick fixes, but fail to deliver the action plan that men need most. My intended audience is small because I am only looking to the overachievers that are committed with their lives. Few of the fatherhood titles I have read over the years have been practically useful for long-term success. Most of them are written assuming that you are an idiot who has made a careless mistake. They discount the fact that some of us are intent on being in a thriving relationship and want to build a strong family. Some of these books attempt to make the promise that you can wing it and still stay cool, without disrupting your current life. Many other books are targeted to expectant women and their mothers-in-law, hoping that Dad will wake up and start being responsible. In contrast, I don't expect you to be careless and incapable, nor do I expect you to merely pretend to be someone else when certain people are watching. The goal of those books seems to be to just check a few boxes so everyone will leave you alone to keep enjoying your comic books, video games, poker night, and the non-stop football podcasts. They aim to teach you that you can survive and just stay out of trouble without inconveniencing your current life, which, if we are honest, may be pretty non-productive as a whole. There is also no shortage of books that will give you 100 generic recommendations on little things that you should probably be doing, that would probably help, if you could miraculously remember to do them all. What we all need are a few realistic, proven tactics that produce tangible results. We need tools for real life application. We need accurate expectations and proper planning for long-term success. I've never come across any particular book that represented this ideology and approach to fatherhood, or one that gave me a measurable edge on learning the job quickly. My hope is that these pages will serve as an awakening, a motivation, and an instruction manual for the tasks before you.

The world doesn't need more mediocre men that merely look exceptional on social media. We need you to actually be a model of success. That is to know who you are, to know what to do, to know how to do it, and to deliver on all of your family responsibilities. Looking like you are good at it is pretty easy, considering the contrast to the average adult male. Let's be honest, most of the sperm contributors in the world don't have much of a clue. Baboons and rabbits can become a father pretty easily. Our initial contribution isn't really much to brag about, even if you think you're good at it. Being above average today probably means that you know how to properly spell your child's middle name and remember to buy him something on his birthday. Planning to pay child support if something goes awry isn't an adequate plan. We need to be substantially more prepared for all the rigmarole that comes with this new job. Being baptized in this raging sea that is fatherhood is daunting. The trek over this new territory can seem like an impossibly demanding, and intimidating task, but we can overcome those fears and sentiments. There is much to learn, in so little time, and the platform beneath us changes rapidly and often. Everyone needs a few pointers in the beginning to help them build momentum.

The items in this book are not just unsolicited recommendations; they are refined tactics that have worked for me. They are not the only ways to succeed but are certainly some of the superior ways to do so. Once you hit your stride, you can confidently and successfully take each obstacle, one by one, and pound it. This will be so much more than just hints and warnings on how to merely survive. The chapters that follow will give you the necessary tools and techniques to perform like a pro and to tower above the status quo. Dare I say that you may even like the new position, hold it in higher esteem than becoming the new CEO of your company, and take extreme pride and personal satisfaction in executing it well.

I just want to be upfront and honest about *Hacking Fatherhood*. It's not for everyone. I say this because I know that some people lack the endurance and the self-worth to finish the drill. It's a lot of work, and many are unwilling and unable put in the necessary effort. I'm writing for a few men that are intentional life-learners and honestly dedicated to excellence. The fact that you are reading any book on fatherhood already puts you in the top 90% of all human adults with a penis. So, bravo to you on your willingness to go that far and even consider preparing for the gigantic responsibility that is before you. Don't get cocky, though. We sit in a pretty pathetic crowd. Of the top 10% of men who will actually read any book on fatherhood, I assume that there are only about 10% in that group who sincerely desire to ramp it up and have the character and raw tenacity to execute. These are the guys that don't just want to survive the transition, but absolutely want to rock it, at all costs. These are the ones who don't just have an awareness and a desire to enter fatherhood; they are the ones that will faithfully put in the work to be exceptional at it. Those of you who are relatively sharp have already figured out that I am claiming that this book is only for about 1% of half of the population of the literate world. I hope that my assessment is wrong and that mankind is in better shape than I observe. I expect the number of men that do care will increase as men like you begin to lead by example and educate the world on what real fatherhood is all about. I wish there was some insanely difficult mental and physical task I could give you to determine if you are one of us, like the Navy Seal 'Hell Week' training and elimination process.

When it comes down to it, a lot of men are simply lazy. Some of us don't know it and others are downright proud of it. Some are experts at being mediocre and are admittedly content there. Let's face it: being average these days requires minimal effort or intelligence. Some don't take the job seriously. Some try to invest as little as possible and don't mind being average or even falling below the median. This book is not about scraping by or faking it. *Hacking Fatherhood* is about learning ways to kill it. Its purpose is to expose ways to be efficient, productive, and smarter. It's for the small subgroup of men that will stretch themselves to the limit in order to be exceptional.

This book is packed with insights that will save time, money, energy, and possibly your marriage and social life. However, make no mistake about it, the strategies in this book will require extra work. With knowledge comes responsibility, and doing this fatherhood thing well requires everything that you have. The demanding work is rough sometimes, but you can't call in sick or hire a surrogate when you get tired. It's vitally important to have realistic expectations from the beginning. Let me help with a few now. Doing this process right means that your golf handicap will likely rise. Several hobbies that have been so important in your life will have to take a back seat or totally disappear. It means that you will miss some, or all of the games and outings that you once enjoyed with your core group of friends. It means that you will have to be present for your wife and your child(ren) more often and more intently. You will be sleep-deprived and still expected to get up and be as productive as you were on your best day. Your sex life will take several temporary hits, but in time, will become stronger than ever. Your social life will change dramatically, but in time, will recover. There are no days off. Being a good dad is a lifestyle. It's not a temporary season, but rather a commencement into another permanent phase of life, which means one phase will be left behind. I want you to realize that your entire identity is going to change. This is who we are. We are fathers.

Hacking Fatherhood is not just about possessing rare and elite knowledge. It's about becoming a leader, developing wisdom and tenacity, and building endurance and character. It's about growing as a person and rising to the call before you. We will do this in the smartest, most efficient way possible. Whether she has ever expressed it or not, your wife does desire for you to lead. The entire household is more secure when you are capable and everyone knows that you are. We will not discuss how to pull the sticky tab on a diaper or how to wipe a bottom properly. What we will discover is how we will take pride in these ever so mundane tasks. Let's create a family culture. Let's plow some fertile ground, plant some seeds, and tend to the crop feverishly. We will sample the goods along the way to make sure everyone stays focused and motivated. Then at harvest time, we will feast and celebrate the success from putting in the intense work all season.

Here's the kicker: if you are the type of person that I hope you are, you will take pride in these ideas and ideals. You will actually want to work harder because you understand the gravity of the new vocation. The process will not only be a challenge, but it will also be the very thing that gives you true purpose in life. Learning these fatherhood hacks will give you true satisfaction because you will be slaying the proverbial dragon, becoming a hero, and elevating several people to a higher state of being. I heard someone say, "If you love what you do, it never feels like work." That's bull! You can love fatherhood and make it your number one priority and passion, but you can bet that there will be many times when it feels like work. You may get pounded to the canvas with an unexpected left hook from time to time, but with some gritty, back-alley, informal training, and a will to win, you will never lose by knockout.

My only real credibility for being qualified to write a book like this is that at the time of writing, I have five children of my own. I also have 12 nieces and nephews. My home has had some serious action over the last ten years. We've had seven pregnancies, two miscarriages, one special needs child, and everything in between. That has made for a valuable, nonstop education. My personality lends itself very well to learning on the fly and to developing hacking systems. I have an inability to sit still, an insatiable appetite to learn, and an obsession with productivity, efficiency, and winning. All of these things made for a useful package that is now in front of you. My wife and I have what I consider to be a wonderful marriage and an exceptional family life. I know that these things are a gift, and I cannot take credit for the success in the household. My partner is a super ninja, and I was raised in a very stable, loving household myself. But just so that you can trust me, you should know that I completed tons of homework before ever considering fatherhood and have remained studious throughout the journey. To this day, I still crave to learn more about the vocation. The plan is ever-changing, and the dynamics can shift so dramatically that if you don't learn to pivot quickly, you will get disoriented and lost. I experiment every day. I have a creative mind that loves to problem solve and create new tactics, techniques, and strategies. I have learned a great deal, and it would be selfish not to share these things. That is why this project happened. My goal is not all pious; part of it is also selfish. That's because I really need you to succeed so that the world that my children live in is a better one.

If you are up for it, we'll just jump right in. I have high expectations for you. If you join me on this journey, I promise that I will not insult you with constant references to beer, the toilet seat, or football. I will not try to be cool and relevant by calling you "dude," "homie," or "playa." I will not mindlessly fill pages with extra content just to make it look more impressive and make me look like a real author. We will cover important topics clearly and concisely. This is a functional book for you, not a self-fulfillment project for me. I respect you for considering the journey and hope that this will enrich your life. It's not about you. It's not about me. It's about family, and now is the time.

The Political Correctness Disclaimer:

For the sake of simplicity and brevity, I made a decision to refer to the child in this book as a "he," and to call the woman who is carrying your child your "wife." I know that there are many inclusions and exclusions to take into account on these subjects and that generalizations are taboo (in general). However, it will take too much time to use all of the exceptions and variations every time a man, woman, or child is mentioned. If you are not married, the same systems still apply. If you are having a baby girl or three of them, the rules still work. I'm not discriminating; I'm just impatient. Please forgive me.

Tomorrow is a New Day

If we are given happiness, it's easy to pass it on. If we are experiencing anger and pain, they are even easier to pass on. We transfer attitudes and emotions automatically, unless we make an active choice not to.

Every generation should be better than the previous one. I know that every person reading this has a vastly different story to tell (or adamantly withhold) about their own fathers. If you are like me, your dad did a terrific job, and you want to climb to new heights with your children. On the contrary, if you are someone like my father, your dad wasn't a model example. He may have given you undeniable reasons to be very different so that your children would not be forced to endure any of the same sufferings that you did. Those experiences have motivated you to be so much better for your family. That attitude, Sir, is to be commended. As my father says and practices, "You can choose to be a victim forever, or you can choose to change the future." Indecision is a decision. You want to be the catalyst that starts a positive and permanent chain reaction for family involvement and success that will continue for many generations. Regardless of each unique situation, we should all be tirelessly working towards a higher level of devotion than we were given.

As an uncomfortable side note, if you are bitter and angry with your father, keep working to improve those feelings. Harboring unforgiveness in any relationship can hold you emotionally hostage and cripple your ability to reach full potential. This may seem unfair and terribly difficult to hear, but it's still the truth. An awesome relationship hack is to develop the ability to forgive and to apologize. Very few people master it. There is so much freedom in these gestures, no matter how they are received. The act of doing it, albeit difficult, creates freedom. That freedom enables us to move on and escape the emotional burdens that are present when we are enduring ongoing heartache or abuse in a relationship. Forgiving someone else is a gift to self. We benefit the most when we forgive someone else.

You possess the power to be something amazing for your family or to be something shameful. Regardless of where you have been or what you have done, now is the time to get serious. The only thing that you can control from here is your effort. Let's make sure that component is unwavering. Stay focused, become strong, and keep your head up. Eventually, every storm passes, making way for a brighter day. Time and maturity and can heal many wounds. A diligent pursuit of what is true, loving, and just can cure many ills. We must chase the things of value and give of ourselves every day. In the absence of guilt and shame, while maintaining a sense of satisfying duty, we become the rock that cannot be shaken. The daily problems and hassles that derail many men will not even phase you, because you know who you are. Real love is demanding, but it's the only option for real men.

Real love is putting into action the realization that someone is more important than yourself. You can achieve this virtue with your child regardless of what your parents did or did not do for you. Fatherly love is the act of giving your life for the sake of someone else's needs. Love your wife, and love your (soon-to-be) child. If you love and give it all you have, you elevate them to a higher position. It is in that process that we can find some peace and meaning in our lives. It's important for us to see our work benefitting others, especially those that we care for the most. When near the end of life, many men look back with regret and feelings of failure, knowing that they should have taken the job more seriously. No one ever says, "I wish I had spent less time and effort on my kids." Most men realize the shortcomings and regrets long before they reach their death beds. Hopefully, this realization occurs before irreparable damage has been done. The true measure of a man is his sense of this vocation and more precisely, how he chooses to love. When you do it well, you are respected, and the love is more likely to be reciprocated. As men, we all desire to be respected. We want to hear things like "good job" and "thank you," and while these are all fine and good, the message that we desperately need to receive is, "I'm proud of you." Your child may not say this for 15, 24, or even 55 years, but the only way to increase the probability that it will ever happen is if you stay the course for the duration and give him countless, undeniable reasons to validate you. More importantly, he will see the role of a real man and a real father throughout his life. That example will lead him to be one too. What we choose to do now will affect generations after us.

Part of being a successful father is taking extreme care of our children. The other part of that equation is that we must also take extreme care of their mother. Their mother will be the one person who they probably value above all the rest. We must protect that supreme relationship and foster it whenever possible. Parents play different roles, and two working together in harmony is an amazing force for good. This partnership, or lack of, has the power to change a child's future, for better or worse. We must give these roles the respect and attention they warrant.

I believe there is no such thing as "love at first sight." Infatuation at first sight maybe. But make no mistake about it: love must be cultivated. We have to learn to love our wives. It is a process. Love grows. We get better at it only if we intentionally work to do so. We don't "love" pizza; we simply prefer its taste over another food. Some of us may not really love our wives yet. Like the pizza, we just admittedly prefer them over someone else. Nonetheless, we can learn to love them in a self-giving, sacrificial way. Continuously cultivating more love is the only way to succeed at this family gig. It is a cumulative, sometimes slow process.

We are all in this together. As the adage says, raising children takes a village. Just know that relying on the village, your mom, your mother-in-law, a daycare, or your best bud is not a foolproof plan. Villages burn down. Friends move away. Relatives and trustees pass away. A man can be suddenly left feeling abandoned without the help and support of friends or family. We must learn self-mastery in the rare event that we are deserted by the rest of the village, and our children come to rely on us alone. Even if we never encounter the need to parent solo, we should always be leading our family in a way that prepares for the possibility.

There are no do-overs when it comes to marriage and child-rearing. Every day matters. Every emotion matters. Every moment matters. You can reboot the server sometimes, but you can never completely replace the hard drive and dump the memory. Every decision from here forward carries much weight. There is too much at stake to approach this subject flippantly. Get your game face on.

We will now begin the journey. This book will cover two years' worth of baby prep and one week of on-the-job training after the little one arrives. I know that this schedule seems a little unorthodox, but, in time, it will make sense. To end well, we must start well. This book is about preparing for a successful start and getting off on the right foot. We will begin the timeline at 24 months BC (Before Childbirth) and work our way to one week AD (After Delivery)

It's plausible to think that you have less than 24 months at this point. That may be why you are reading so feverishly now. If you are ahead of the timeline, that's all right. Please don't skip ahead. Every bit of this information is valuable, even if you use it outside of the preferred or ideal stage. You will still be able to use most of this information this time around, but will certainly be able to use it next time, on baby number two. That is, if you do in fact survive this round and have enough amnesia to go for it again. I have confidence that you will do just that.

24 MONTHS BC (BEFORE CHILD)

How to Get Pregnant… It's Harder Than You Think

It was the best season of my life, a remarkably euphoric time. Sex was happening daily, and I didn't even have to earn it or convince her that it was a good idea.

So, you have decided that you want to have a baby. Most relationships start by actively trying to prevent a baby, then transition into casually not preventing anymore, and intending to just "let it happen." Eventually, if merely being open for business doesn't produce any results, couples may start deliberately trying to have a baby. The first few months of trying are a lot of fun, especially for the guys. For most of us, we are regularly getting to do the very thing that we think about 8,000 times per day. I think that stat may be a little high. Every seven seconds? Really? That number has got to be off by at least 10%. Nonetheless, most guys won't have any trouble obliging their spouse when she is requesting, or demanding, the sacred ritual. I said, "the first few months" for a reason. The truth is, after a few months of unsuccessful trying, some new attitudes tend to crash the party. By this point, the guy is often in a blissful, almost unconscious routine. Sexual intoxication has become his new baseline, and he's much less observant to real marriage behavior and needs. He may have lost a sense of reality and might be getting pretty spoiled. Planning the next session in his head, he begins missing the normal relationship signals. In stark contrast to his lack of focus, she is now starting to worry. She is upset that it hasn't happened yet and is now questioning, probably for the first time, if everything is working properly. She is worried about you, about her, and about the future. Has she done something wrong? Have you?

In most cases, the trying continues with no change in schedule or methods, and the intended results remain unremarkably unchanged. That is, she doesn't get pregnant, and you keep going hoping the same tactics will produce a different result. After a few more months, things start to get emotionally unstable. For the first time, it's starting to feel like work, not play. Your supportive reassurance doesn't seem to help as your loved one spirals into a sedated, worrisome, mental fog that never breaks. After 9 to 12 months, hopelessness sets in, and she wants to see a doctor. Now what? Most times, everything checks out fine with both parties. Sometimes an issue is discovered that needs to be treated or helped along, but most of the time the couple is left with the advice that they should just try more. This sequence is all too common but ALL wrong.

Two major problems plague couples when they are trying for the first time. One is that our expectations are usually way off. The other is that our technique is nowhere close to right. I think our expectations are off because of a simple lack of conversation. For whatever reasons, this is not a subject that comes up over dinner with friends. Women don't want to talk about the difficulty they are having getting pregnant.

It's like this entire subject is just out of bounds. It makes people feel like they are failing. Guys certainly aren't talking about it. They aren't talking about anything. The assumption is that everyone else got pregnant as soon as they were ready because we never heard otherwise. The truth is that it is very common to be trying for 12+ months. It's typically not even considered a potential infertility issue until after a year of unsuccessful attempts. A year of unsuccessful attempts should be the normal expectation, but again, no one ever talks about this. Everyone's expectations are incorrectly framed from a lack of accurate information.

For women that have been using artificial means to prevent pregnancy for years, it could likely take even longer to become pregnant. Her system needs to recover from the physical, hormonal, and chemical stress it has been under for years. I think it's a lot to ask for a woman to endure this chemical barrage, while we demand so little of men. I know that my stance on artificial birth control being unfair to women is rare, but maybe it's worth explaining further. These pills take a healthy working system and influence parts of it to stop working. I think medicine should make a poorly functioning system work better, not make a perfectly good one shut down. The list of side effects is nauseating, and some of the risks are tremendous. Is it fair to expect women to deal with all of the burdens and all of the responsibility? It's an accepted practice because most people think it's the norm, but is it the best option? I know that some will think that I'm an alien, and this single paragraph may get me in trouble. I'm not trying to judge anyone. However, I do want you to think about alternatives that could be less noxious. Study all the methods and all the potential risks. Choose the best option for your wife, her sanity, and her health, even if it requires more work and discipline for you. I can tell you definitively that the men I know that decided not to demand this of their wives have seen immediate benefits in their marriages. Their wives appreciated it and loved getting off the meds. Those benefits are diverse, including physical, emotional, and sexual improvements. My wife and I do not use artificial birth control, and never have. For what it's worth, I do practice what I preach on this topic.

Hopefully, a full recovery to a healthy system ensues after a cease in medicine. That transition back to normal function is not typically immediate, especially if certain parts of her system haven't functioned naturally in several years. For people who have not been preventing with drugs, trying to get pregnant will likely be a faster process. Again, I'm not trying to start a fight or point fingers. I'm just seeking to frame some accurate expectations. It takes a while for most everyone to get pregnant, and it can take even longer if menstrual cycles have been interrupted for some time. Hormone levels have to stabilize to healthy levels again, and powerful chemicals have to be processed out of the system.

The common but troublesome delay in achieving pregnancy is natural and should be expected. So many small things have to happen in perfect timing to get pregnant. Even if you know the exact hour of peak fertility, it can still be a long shot. When you are just blindly guessing, it's almost impossible. The expectation should be that it takes many months. You only get one really high percentage try per month. If you are lucky, you get two good chances. When we have *tried*

30 times, and it doesn't happen, even though only one of them was actually a well-timed, viable try, it can feel impossible and hopeless. The real truth is that it's not as bad as you think. You were really 0 for 1, not 0 for 30. The other 29 were not legitimate, educated tries. The problem is that you didn't know that your timing was way off the mark. We must change the math in order to change the expectations and the success rate. Don't worry, I am not going to restrict you to just two sessions per month. Where is the fun in that? Besides, I know that you are needier than that. I am too.

So, what about technique? I'm not trying to deflate your man prowess or cause your bowed chest to deflate during the one time of your life that you are actually enjoying your work. I'm sure that your technique is fine, Mr. Stallion. I am referring to the schedule. The technique of going for the gusto every chance you get is fun, but it's also wrong. It's true that if you do the deed every day, that you are bound to hit a day with good ovulation and high fertility. However, you are still unlikely to get the desired result, which is conception, right? Getting accurate information on how timing and technique affect your success rate is paramount. There are two components to this that people discount or don't even consider. These two things are simple: her schedule and his schedule. Now is a good time for a little bit of education. If you know how it all works, you can dramatically increase your chances of success. I am amazed at guys on the golf course that have been playing the game almost weekly for ten years, that still can't break 90, and still have the same dreadful slice that they had a decade ago. They never take time to diagnose the problem, to learn the mechanics, and then skillfully work on a smart solution to fix the problem. They just expect that with enough practice, it will work itself out and a desirable outcome will one day just appear. Unfortunately, hitting more balls the same way, over and over, doesn't usually help—no pun intended!

Let's talk about science for a minute. I hope you remember from your 10th-grade biology class that a single sperm must reach a viable egg for this pregnancy thing to work. If your swimmers are kicking like Michael Phelps, but their numbers are too few, they might not make it there. If there are a legion of Lochtes all doing it right, but there is no viable egg, they can't hit the mark to finish the job. So how do you know when the time is right? Let's just focus on her first. After all, she has way more of a physical investment in this entire ordeal than you do. What an understatement! Lucky for all of us, there are some definitive ways to know if and when she is ovulating. You've probably heard of the calendar, or the rhythm method, which is simply counting days. This helps, but it's not foolproof by any means. Let's start with that. From day one of her menstrual cycle (when her period starts and bleeding begins), you can start counting days to know what is happening internally. By day seven, an egg is ripening in a typical ovulatory cycle. Usually, between 7-11 days from the start day, the uterus begins to thicken, and cervical fluids change. After 11 days, hormones begin to change, which cause a healthy egg to be released and become available. This release is called ovulation and is when all systems are a go for conception. This magical day of human physiology should take place on the middle day of the cycle. The literature will say that this release typically happens on day 14. The problem is that all of this is based on having a totally predictable cycle that is the ideal 28 days, every month, every time. That certainly doesn't represent all women. It might not even be anywhere in the ballpark for your gal. The problem with the calendar method is that if a woman has a cycle of 19 days or 42 days, and varies each month, the counting is futile and unreliable. It is now, once again, just a guessing game. The other complicated issue is that several outside factors may affect the patterns. Illness, medications, lack of sleep, nutrition, physical problems, emotional issues, and good ole fashioned stress can all affect her cycle timing and cause variations within it.

It should comfort you to know that some of the aforementioned ovulation cycle changes can be accurately monitored. That means that you don't have to rely on counting alone, which is not typically sufficient. Each change of the monthly cycle is accompanied by hormonal changes that can be measured. One easy way to monitor these changes is with a fertility monitor. This modern marvel is a handheld digital device that tests for rises in hormones, usually luteinizing hormone (LH) or estrogen. It's compact, about the size of your old iPhone 4 (not your iPhone 6 Plus). The woman provides a urine sample on a test stick, which is loaded into the machine, to test her hormone levels. This is done at home and doesn't require a trip to the doctor's office. When the hormones spike, we know that ovulation is starting and an egg is soon-to-be released. The machine will show you about six days of fertility increase, and identify one or two peak days when fertility is the highest. Your spouse will check the machine every morning to see if a test is indicated. The monitor asks for many tests the first month to learn her cycle, then will only request a test sample on the more likely fertile days in following months. These simple devices cost around

$200, and the test sticks are about a buck each. There are also separate, less expensive, single-use ovulation testing sticks that don't require a monitor. The disposable stick just shows a one-time reading. If you want to cover all the bases, at all costs, get the monitor. It provides more peace of mind because it gives more feedback, more instructions, and tracks more data. If you want to stay with the low-budget option and just want to feel better about expectations, use the single test sticks. Add this method to your bag of tricks as another adjunct tool to use in learning which days are best to release the hounds.

Beyond counting days and digital hormone testing, there are even more ways to monitor, learn, and know the peak ovulation days. You will be happy to know that the rest of the methods are free. See, other changes to a woman's body also point to a clearer picture of what is happening and when. There are temperature changes that show trackable patterns if you take her temperature the same time each morning. Relax, I mean her oral temperature. There are also definitive changes to her cervix that provide distinct ovulation information. This fascinating body part is a tube-like section of tissue that sits in between her uterus and her vagina. In simple terms, it's like a gate. The cervix changes position by moving up and down throughout the cycle. It also opens and closes to allow a more direct pathway to the new viable egg. Once your lady learns the right way to check her cervix, using her finger, she can very accurately know what it's doing. The position, firmness, and openness all tell you what stage of the cycle she is in, and therefore what comes next. There are also changes in the consistency of fluids inside her feminine parts. Again, once she learns the right way to check and test herself, these mucous patterns point us to even more useful information. Her body temperature, cervix activity, and internal fluids are all working together to provide a more accommodating environment that makes sperm live longer. These changes also make for easier travel for your tadpoles, so they can hopefully have better odds to get the job done. When working properly, her system wants to get pregnant every month. Everything in her body starts catering to the possibility. Not coincidentally, this will also be the time of the month when she most desires sexual activity. Even cooler, it will also be the time you are most attracted to her and really want to do the deed because of crazy chemicals, hormones, pheromones, signs, and signals that are happening without you even knowing it. I find all of these changes fascinating. It's incredible that this epic cycle happens every month!

That information should be enough to get you excited and to peak your interest in the subject. I hope you will dig even deeper into all of this. This book is not meant to be a comprehensive guide for teaching you everything about measuring her fertility. There is a wealth of knowledge available on this subject. Search for books on "Natural Family Planning" (NFP) and read reviews. You could probably get the info for free on blogs. (P.S. Authentic Catholics are usually the best resource for this education. Find a Catholic mom's guide to NFP.) Now that you are more equipped, let's press on.

As I said, your wife will have to learn and monitor a few of these things on her own and just let you know of the findings. Using an "all of the above" approach in the beginning is good. Track everything that is trackable for a few months until you start to get a good picture. In time, you will only need to actively watch one or two of the items and probably won't even need the monitor anymore. The other great thing about learning how to read all these signs is that this same system will become your all-natural form of birth control in the times when you are spacing children or do not wish to conceive. This is Natural Family Planning for both conception and contraception. My wife and I have practiced it for 14 years without any mishaps. All four of our children were planned and intended. The system really works, plus there is no bloating, cramping, increase in the risk of cancer, weight gain, sleep problems, hormonal rages, blindness, anal bleeding, foaming at the mouth, loss of sexual desire, or any of the other side effects you hear on the commercials. Plus, it's a lot cheaper than visiting the pharmacy every month.

OK, back to your part. It's simple, really. This is a numbers game. You only need one sperm to make it to the fertile egg. When you have sex, you typically release over 100 million. The more you have to release, the better your chances. So how do you increase the payload? The truth is that it takes time to build up a good supply of mature sperm. As they say, "abstinence makes the sperm grow stronger." OK, no one says that, but it's true. And yes, I did just use the A-word. If you are having sex daily or releasing in other ways, your numbers are not fully recovering. So instead of trying to have sex every night during the "trying to get pregnant" phase, hold off for a few days in between sessions. Every other day or every third day is recommended. If you track her patterns for a few months and get the hang of the system, save up for two days before peak day, and then let it rip. I mentioned that her hormonal rages are likely to cease when she stops taking pills, but your hormonal rage will take some work. Breathe. You can do this. It will get easier once you realize that you can, in fact, abstain for a day or two without imploding. If you want to do it the natural way, it takes some self-control. Everything in life that has any value takes discipline. Getting everything you want, whenever you want, makes you a spoiled jerk. Take one for the team every now and then. It won't kill you, and your selfless gestures will be rewarded with more intimacy. Intimacy is something that few couples have, but everyone is haphazardly longing for.

Common knowledge says that we should all have a healthy diet and get plenty of exercise to maintain optimal health. Strive to be as healthy as possible. It matters physically and mentally. If you wear briefs or boxer briefs, switch to boxers for the time when you are trying to get pregnant. Or heck, just go commando. It's good for the soul every now and then anyway. Temperature is an issue for your testes. Your boys drop lower to try to stay cool. Your warm body temperature actually kills sperm. Wearing briefs or otherwise tight pants keeps them too close to your body and overheats them. So, eat well, exercise, and keep the jewels cool for several weeks to get the desired results. A few more things to consider: many lubricants, jams, and jellies that promise to increase performance and transform both of you into sex-crazed maniacs have chemicals in them that kill sperm. Check your labels. Saliva from either party can also be a detriment to sperm health.

If you know that the time is right, take advantage of the opportunity. You may get a, "Honey, you forgot your lunch and need to come home and get it," call at work one day. I guess nowadays you would get an otherwise weird text message with phallic emoticons of bananas, flowers, and chicken eggs. She may hastily dismiss your buddies unusually early one evening, insisting to them that you "have a lot to do and really need your rest." One time, I had just driven an hour back home after leaving my wife visiting at her parents' house when she called and said that she just realized that she was at peak fertility and needed my services stat. I returned because I do take pride in my job. It had to be pretty odd for the family to see me return just a few hours after having left, have a seemingly important private conversation in the back, only to then leave again shortly, (cough…) I mean a long time, after. Another incident was quite memorable. Years ago, I went on an overnighter to compete in an adventure race with my best buddy, Jay. My wife also went to support our team and cheer us on. To save money, the three of us decided to lodge together. Yep, you guessed it. All the signs aligned the night before the 6:00 a.m. starting race time. It was peak fertility time, and we were in the process of actively trying to have a baby. She creatively got my race partner to go out to fetch some item that she urgently needed from the Dollar General while I was in the shower. As soon as he left, we did our thing. It was a great weekend! We won the adventure race, defeating 20 teams in an epic comeback story, and successfully conceived our first child. We named him General after the Dollar General down the street. Just kidding!

20 MONTHS BC

Lies and Logistics

It's going to cost how much? How the heck did that guy afford it... five times?

Great news! This chapter is worth between $3,000 and $30,000. Seriously! The not-so-great news is that to get the reward, you have to take a crash course in health insurance. I know this isn't anyone's favorite topic, but it's extremely valuable. The most logical place to start the insurance discussion is in the awesomely ignorant and blissful time of paternal consideration. You know, when you think you want to become a dad. This is a fun time for couples to start romanticizing about what it will be like to have a child of their own. I think we all like to imagine life with a small child and all the fun things we will do together. We dream about the exciting and fulfilling experiences we will share with our little buddies. Staying up all night and getting puked on is usually not part of the fantasy. The truth is that kids are not real fun immediately. The visions we have are usually playing with kids that are several years old. We will get to those years, but for now, let's back up a bit.

If you are open to the idea of becoming a parent, and maybe even leaning towards liking the idea, there are a few things that you need to master. Number one on the list is knowing about typical expenses and insurance jargon. Most people know that having a baby is expensive. For the birth alone, you can expect to pay between $3,000 and $12,000. These are the doctors' fees and hospital charges if everything goes perfectly and the process doesn't get unexpectedly complicated. If there is a glitch or deviation in the ideal plan, like a C-section, the need for a high-risk doctor, or complications with the baby, there is no limit to how high that number may climb. If Mom or baby needs extra medicines, tests, or other services, the bill can rapidly start to swell. Your world will be totally rocked when a baby comes, and there will be plenty of stress. There is no need to add financial stress on top of it all. Preparation and expectation are keys to hacking this piece of the puzzle. You will need to do your best to put away money now, every month, so that you have $5,000-10,000 in the bank or your Health Savings Account (HSA) when the time comes. Don't worry, I'm going to teach you how to keep most of the saved funds. I know the topic of insurance and savings sounds boring, but stick with me.

Insurance preparation must come early, even before considering pregnancy. Why? Because it only takes nine months to incubate a tiny human, but most insurance companies have a 12-month waiting period before they will provide maternity coverage. The Affordable Care Act supposedly eliminated waiting periods, but it's just a duck and cover scheme. Technically, there are no waiting periods, but you can only purchase coverage during select periods of "open enrollment" during the year, which inevitably creates a new type of waiting period. There is no such thing as a free lunch when it comes to health insurance. If it sounds too good to be true, it probably is. This legislation promised a great deal but didn't deliver on those promises. You will still likely have to pay for many extra months of coverage for just a few months of use. You must also remember that there is more to maternity coverage than just the delivery and hospital fees. The prenatal care also typically accounts for several thousand dollars of the total cost of having a baby. Those fees may be charged in addition to the ones listed previously. So, it might not be that you need just 9 months of insurance coverage before delivery; you may actually need 12 months on the insurance plan before even becoming pregnant and starting prenatal care. That means you may need to start paying premiums 21 months before the planned birth date to cover the 12-month wait, plus the 9 months of care after the waiting period, before the delivery. Buzzkill, I know!

The frustrating problem with health insurance is that every company differs, every plan within that company differs, and every medical facility differs. Beyond the insurance plan and what you think they cover, every doctor's office and hospital differ in how they charge fees and when they do so. I know, this is a frustrating pain in your rear, but it will save you massive amounts of money, so it's worth the time. I have a simple approach to solve these problems for you. This stage will require some homework to ensure that there are no surprises. No one wants a $5,000 surprise expense.

Every couple fits into one of these categories. First, let's identify the category you are currently in. Then follow the steps to properly hack this issue and prevent unforeseen trouble.

Category A: Your wife currently has medical insurance.

Find out if maternity coverage is already on her plan. If it is, find out how long the policy has been in effect and how long the waiting period is for maternity coverage, to make sure you are in the clear. If she has coverage and has passed the waiting period, you are almost all set. Just call the facilities that you plan to be using for care and make sure that they accept your plan. If she doesn't have coverage for maternity on her current plan, find out what it costs to add it and what the time constraints are. Also, make sure than your preferred doctor and hospital accept this specific plan. Don't ask if they accept the insurance company, ask if they accept the exact plan.

Category B: She doesn't have medical insurance, and you do.

Find out if she is on your current plan. If she isn't on your policy, find out what it takes to add her to the plan. Determine what maternity options are there for coverage and find out if there any specific limits on the coverage.

Category C: Neither of you has medical insurance, or she cannot be added to your plan.

Find out options for getting her a private insurance plan with maternity coverage. Healthcare.gov is a starting point, but likely not the final destination. You will probably achieve better results going to individual medical insurance companies' websites and using a search tool there. Humana, Blue Cross, and Aetna are some of the larger providers. I recommend talking to friends and family to find out what plans they are on and if there were any surprises or pitfalls using them.

For all three of the situations above, there are additional options, but we must first consider traditional insurance.

This information gathering stage can be a time-consuming task. You must call these companies and find out what is covered by the plans, how much it costs, and what the limitations are. Ask questions until you understand. You cannot determine what the most cost-effective option is until you get all of the information in front of you. If you live in the U.S. and the Affordable Care Act still exists at the time you are reading this, the government healthcare marketplace website is probably a good place to start. Search there to see some options, then dig further into each option by calling the companies that offer the plans. If you are a high-income earner, you will find that you don't get any help and you are expected to pay exorbitant premiums. The current system punishes you. Sorry. The hard truth is that you aren't just paying for your family. You will, in essence, be paying for six or eight people who pay nothing. Again, no such thing as a free lunch. Once you have a clear understanding of deductibles, maximums, coverage amounts, and waiting periods, then you must determine if your providers accept these insurance plans, and if they are in-network for them. Call the obstetrician's (OB) office that you plan to use and ask them what plans have the best coverage and which ones they accept.

An additional option to consider is funding an HSA (Health Savings Account). This is a tax-advantaged savings account that you build up over time and use only for medical expenses. The same account can be used for medical, dental, vision, and pharmacy expenses. You just have to report how much money was deposited into it and how much was removed for medical expenses at tax time each year. The benefit is that you get tax deductions for using this type of account. The only way to participate in the HSA with the tax benefits is to be enrolled in an approved, high-deductible medical insurance plan. Personally, I like this route and use it myself. Since it's a high-deductible plan, that means that insurance coverage will only start once your total bill exceeds the deductible amount. This also means that you will need at least that amount saved in an account. Hopefully, you have an emergency fund stashed away somewhere. If not, start putting money into a savings account every month. Like, go do it right now. I encourage you to make these deposits an automated monthly event so that it happens without you needing to physically do anything. Your bank can set this up with no cost to you. If you bank online, there is probably a simple form on the bank website to do these sorts of transfers. This automated saving system is a life hack, not just a childbirth hack. Everyone needs to put away cash for a rainy day or an emergency. Having a decent amount stashed away creates security and peace of mind.

Back to the HSA plans. Some of these plans do not have maternity coverage, so look closely and be sure to get the right one. These plans are helpful when you have some money in savings and you just want to prevent BIG bills or a catastrophic hospital visit. The hard reality is that you will pay for the delivery one way or another. You will pay it in premiums for an insurance plan that covers it, or you will pay for the portion that the cheaper plan doesn't cover. It's expensive, unless you qualify for some assistance from the state, from a federal plan, from an employer, or from the hospital itself. The key is having protection from unforeseen events that you could not afford to pay if something goes badly wrong. Staying in the hospital for extended periods, having surgery, or receiving prolonged treatments can quickly get ridiculously expensive.

So, what's the right option? If you can get on an existing plan with a spouse or join a policy at work, that's likely the best option, as the employer pays part of the premiums. If you are on your own, it's different. On your own, if you have a routine pregnancy and delivery with zero complications, you are much better off just paying for the services outright (with the negotiated discount techniques that I will show you later in the book) and not using any insurance. In other words, by the time you pay premiums for 12 months (waiting period) + another 9 months (pregnancy and delivery), you would likely have been able to afford to pay cash for the whole thing anyway and come out better on the total. You just need to do the math. However, if you go with the uninsured route to save money, it's risky. If you don't have coverage, and something non-routine happens, the prenatal hospital bills can skyrocket. These events are exactly what insurance is for. If your spouse becomes high-risk during pregnancy because of placenta previa, preeclampsia, twins, low birth weight baby, or any other issues, you will need to see a specialist, which will certainly cost more. If you need a C-section instead of a vaginal birth, the bills just went way up again. A single extra night in the hospital can add thousands to your bill. An extra few days can get ugly real quickly. Obviously, the problem is that there is no way to predict these things. That is why you should be prepared and have some coverage in place for the worst case scenarios.

There is one other item that is imperative for you to understand. Once the baby is born, he will be on his own plan. If there is a problem, and the new addition has to spend eight days in the NICU (Neonatal Intensive Care Unit) at the hospital, that stay is not typically classified as a maternity service. Once the little one enters the world, he will have his own patient record and his own set of bills. If you have an active insurance plan in place, you just call the insurance company (usually within 30 days) and add the new addition to the plan as soon as you have a Social Security number for him. The services provided to him would be retroactively covered as long as you get the policy soon enough. In the case of a high-deductible HSA plan, the deductible is usually a family combined deductible. Again, make sure that you understand your deductible, her deductible, and if they will be combined under a family deductible.

I know this topic stinks and is starting to irritate you and cause anxiety, but stick with me for a few more minutes. We're almost done. This final part is a downer too, but again, very valuable to understand. If you presently have or later obtain coverage, don't assume that the policy is what it says that it is. The website will say that it pays 80% of labor and delivery, but that doesn't mean that it will pay 80% of what the hospital charges. Most people don't realize this deceptive truth. The insurance company pays 80% of a preset amount that the insurance company thinks is a fair price based on their pre-set fee schedule, not what the hospital charges. So if a procedure is $1,000 at the hospital or OB office, and the insurance company thinks the procedure limit should be $750, they pay $600 (80% of $750), not $800 (80% of $1,000). Oh, and don't forget, that's after the deductible has been met. Guess who is expected to make up the difference? YOU! So it's imperative that you ask questions when shopping for plans.

Get as much information as possible from the doctors, hospitals, and pharmacies about what the bottom line looks like. Don't just read a form or browse a chart online. Call the company and speak with a knowledgeable person. That in itself can be difficult. If you find a helpful, knowledgeable, polite employee, ask for her name and a direct number. Heck, send some chocolates if you can. You will need a go-to person like that on your team in the future. One of the most important details of the insurance plan is the out-of-pocket maximum. Regardless of how much the insurance plan pays or refuses to cover, you need to know what the maximum amount that you could possibly owe. Keep in mind that there is usually a separate entity that will bill for services by each office or department, like the hospital, doctor, anesthesia, radiology, labs, etc. You need to make sure that all of them accept your plan so that they all combine and contribute to the deductible and the out-of-pocket maximum.

The bottom line is that having good insurance is expensive, and not having insurance is also expensive. I think it's illegal not to have any coverage nowadays, but I'm not sure if Washington D.C. has figured out a way to monitor, enforce, or punish the crime. If you don't have cash stockpiled somewhere, start now and keep adding to it, even if you have great insurance. If you have plenty of cash saved, you still need a plan to help protect the family in case of complications and unexpected services that may skyrocket the numbers by tens or hundreds of thousands of dollars. Even IF you don't read this entire book, please listen to me right here. There is a major money hack and something that few people ever know or practice later in this book.

DO NOT make any payments for medical services for mother or baby until you read the chapter on negotiating and paying bills. In that chapter, I will teach you how to negotiate and reduce every bill. Fifteen minutes on those tactics will save thousands of hard-earned dollars.

Whew, that's enough for now. I'll talk to you about how to negotiate fees and the right way to go about paying for all this in a later chapter. For now, start determining what option is best for your family as it relates to monthly budget and risk tolerance. Preparation is key. Knowledge is power. Surprises stink.

15 MONTHS BC

How to Build a Superhuman

Sometimes we like to poison our kids, just a tiny bit at a time. You know, to make ourselves feel better. Discipline is such an inconvenience to our busy lives.

Disclaimer: I know that this chapter may offend some, but I am confident that most people who would fit into the offended category probably don't read books like this one, so we will trudge forward and hope for the best. I am not trying to be unsympathetic or overly-aggressive, just honest. I'm confident that even if it makes you irritated, you will agree with me, and maybe even find it in your heart to thank me one day.

We want the best for our children, right? Parents will unconsciously say things like, "I'll do anything for my kids," or "My kids are my number one priority." It's much easier to say these things than to practice them. I guess it makes people feel better if they say it out loud. If we look at their schedule and their bank statement, we may see a different priority than what is readily spoken. No one wants to admit their own selfish desires taking precedence over that of a child's needs. It's unlikely that you have ever heard someone say, "I'll do anything for my children… except change my diet, wear cheaper shoes, drive a beater car, and stop smoking." The truth is that some will *do anything* as long as it doesn't require working harder on a marriage, forfeiting favorite purchases, or adding more effort or expense. We don't hear anyone admit it, but this attitude is, all too often, true. We could go into a hundred different required sacrifices that are necessary for a family to thrive, but this chapter is focused on the physical health of the entire household. Hacking physical health, like all other success, requires some preparation. Hacking a new child's health starts with you.

Two of the most important elements to total health, in any stage of life, are rest and nutrition. These only come with deliberate and disciplined systems. When a baby arrives, every area of your life is shaken. An entire new way of life is demanded when a totally dependent newborn shows up on the scene. If you want to really be good at handling these life changes, it's necessary to work out the bugs many months in advance. Rigid schedules and fortified boundaries must be constructed early if we are to prevent the chaos that ransacks so many homes.

The only way to provide optimal nutrition for the bun in the oven is for the new mama to eat an ideal balance of real food. When I say real food, I mean something natural that came out of the ground or had a mother. Furthermore, these food items have not been reconstructed, modified, or fortified in an effort to make them an attractive neon color, kill pests, make them super sweet, super cheap, or prevent them from ever decomposing in a box the way that real food should. The only way for Mom, the developing baby, and the later newborn baby to get optimal nutrition is for the entire household to subscribe to a better way of living. More specifically, the family needs an optimal method of eating well and staying fit, and that certainly includes you. When I said in the beginning pages of this book that this wasn't for everyone and that it would be a life change, I was serious. If you aren't there already, now is the time in your life when you get serious about nutrition. Diets and fads don't ever work because they are temporary. Wellness is a lifestyle, and it must be non-negotiable if you are serious about your role as a family leader. It's time to take the plunge and do it the right way, for the whole family. You are the one to lead the revolution in your house. Without you participating, and preferably leading, it cannot be sustained. Your family needs you for this. Do it for the baby, do it for your wife, and do it for yourself. Everyone wins when you execute the plan well. It's time to start moving more, eating better, and dropping the bad habits. If either of you almost-parents smoke, you gotta kick it. If you eat poorly, now is the time to change that. If the most exercise you get is walking to the refrigerator, you need to start an intentional workout program. I'm not saying that you go all the way from couch zero to CrossFit Games hero today, but it needs to at least start today. Add a healthy practice that is attainable, like working out one more day a week. Once that is routine, add another step. It takes time.

This discussion is about more than just eating well so that the developing baby has all the vitamins and minerals he needs. That alone should be enough to make you want to change your life. We know that Mom is eating for two, and that the growing child can only have access to what she eats. Mom needs to be healthy so the baby can be healthy. We get it. But there's more to it than just child development! Here is where the hacking comes into play.

There are some groundbreaking food studies on babies' nutrition and habits during childhood that are directly linked to the mother's food choices while pregnant. Yes, what she eats while pregnant affects the baby's eating habits after delivery. We know the immune system develops better with better nutrition, and so do the other systems and internal organs that are being formed. What is fascinating and extremely useful for developing the baby's eating habits is that the same foods that mothers consume end up being the ones more preferred by the baby as he grows. What an amazing parenting hack! We can teach a child how to eat before we ever pick up a spoon or a sippy cup. What a gift for your baby. We can actually pre-program them to like good food instead of bad food. If Mom eats a lot of spinach while pregnant and/or breastfeeding, the baby will likely have more of an affinity for spinach in the early years and beyond. If she gorges on doughnuts with icing and sprinkles every morning, she just set up your child for some future struggles with the very same sugary vises. One hard truth that no one wants to admit is that childhood (type 2) diabetes, which was once called adult-onset diabetes, is an illness almost exclusively caused by poor choices. Some parents are actually giving their children diabetes by pre-conditioning them to love sugar, and constantly giving it to them as they grow. In my mind, this is a form of unconscious child abuse. This is too much guilt to ever bear, so let's just avoid it. Also, life is hard enough without unwanted addictions. Don't force your child into a compromised disadvantage by gifting them a sugar addiction. It has been proven that in young infants and toddlers, greens and other healthy vegetables are turned away more by babies who did not receive them in breast milk. But now we know that it's not just breast milk. Further studies have shown the same results for babies in utero, based on Mom's diet, even before breast milk, and even in kids that are exclusively formula fed. So even if you bottle feed your newborn, if Mom ate well while pregnant, the child will prefer better food and be less likely to dislike them later. This hack only works if we commit to doing it early enough. This is like retirement planning in that it's pretty easy to come out ahead if you start correctly and put in work early enough, but it's a mountain to climb and tons of work if you miss the early steps.

My kids are living proof of this. They eat raw veggies like they're going out of style. They also think a six-ounce, non-colored, organic juice box is an amazing luxury. Other parents say things like, "Man, I wish mine would eat a salad like yours do." They assume that we are just lucky, that we won the genetic lottery, and they were unfairly punished. They have no idea that is was an early and deliberate conditioning hack. There is a major soapbox speech that I could give about who buys the groceries and who runs the house, but no one wants to hear that. For the sake of brevity, I will remind you of something embarrassingly obvious. Your two-year-old can't eat Skittles or drink Mountain Dew unless you purchase them and then hand it over. He cannot be approved for a debit card and go shopping. People will make passive aggressive comments about your child's eating habits, but no one will ever commend you on being smart and disciplined, unless they are gloating with you in the same success. My kids each have their favorites and all have different tastes, but they eat what their parents eat at every meal. We all eat real, healthy food. Avocados, broccoli, brussels sprouts, tomatoes, cucumbers, peppers, asparagus, and every fruit you can think of, are all on the weekly menu for all of us. (A lot of this is grown in our own garden... #GroceryHack #FinanceHack). Sure, we have our moments of defiance and coercion when introducing new foods. But you can bet your wallet that my wife has never said, "Lil' Dallas is such a picky eater. He will only eat fried chicken strips, gummy bears, and cheesy fries." I'm sure they would like these things, but they are not available, and therefore, are not missed. Their systems learned early what real foods they will eat. They also indirectly learned what not to eat. For the first few years before we got the grandparents fully on board with the no-junk, all-natural foodie thing, they gave lots of treats and sweets to the boys. That's what grandparents do, right? The ones in our family did too, for a little while anyway. Before we got a handle on the junk food and treats, our kids would come home from an overnight visit with grandparents and actually be sick. They would be lethargic all day once they returned home, probably from the sugar crash. Their little engines were wrecked from the malnutrition. Many times they would actually vomit. Their bodies were rejecting the junk food that was invading their healthy, well-trained systems. It reminded me of the scene in the *Supersize Me* documentary when Morgan Spurlock eats his first value meal from McDonalds and pukes before he finished the fries. Prior to the binge, he was a vegan and a real food consumer. Even if you are late to the game, you can still train them to eat the right things, but it's a whole lot easier if you start pre-pregnancy and if the whole family is on board. Work smarter, not harder. The smart approach on the front end is way easier to pull off than trying to fix these same problems with a defiant two-year-old in the high chair at your favorite restaurant. Everyone benefits with healthier bodies, better rest, more energy, and a sense of well-being.

I do want to take one moment to recognize that some children have mental and physical problems that make certain tastes and smells unbearable. This is the case with many children on the autism spectrum and in kids dealing with other sensory and psychological issues. These special situations should always be approached carefully, with the help of a professional. I know first-hand how impossibly challenging sensory disorders can be. I battle them every day with one of my sons, and it's exhausting and very defeating at times.

The time to start consuming useful foods that benefit our bodies is now. Instead of chowing down on empty calories with zero health value, we must start eating real food that our bodies need to thrive. As a society, we consume huge amounts of sugar and our grocery stores are crammed full of products that have no nutritional value. There is nothing beneficial in so much of what we call food. In case no one else is bold enough to ever say it, I want to make this statement now. No one, especially a child, ever needs to consume a soft drink. It's sugar, dye, and lab chemicals that make you fat, destroy your pancreas, and rot your teeth. Diet drinks may me missing the sugar, but what else is in there? There is nothing of value. Why are these lab-made colas ever acceptable to put in front of people we love? If you want the best for yourself and your child, don't buy this garbage. Tell Grandma too. There is just no need to even introduce these as options to kids. They don't need to be in the house for any of you. A recent study reported that in a day, the average child age 12-18 drinks more calories than they eat. I see kids every week in my dental practice that have $1200 worth of dental treatment needs before their seventh birthday. This is parental abuse and neglect. We are the ones buying the groceries and placing them in front of the kids. This harmful, sugary overload is totally preventable, and the alternative is way cheaper. Drink water. Some juice is OK, but not necessary for daily thriving. Get naturally flavored drinks if you need any additives.

There are also many milk options that aren't full of sugar, preservatives, and hormones. Read the labels and be blown away. Sugar is powerfully addictive. Avoid it. Yes, people will think you are an alien when you bring your own organic juice box and cake to the birthday party instead of partaking in the bright blue sugar and test tube concoction that is offered to all the little tikes. Get over it. Recently, my boy #3 asked if he could get some of the bright candy that was strategically positioned at his eye level in the checkout aisle. Before I could respond, his brother, boy #2, said, "No way! That has chemicals in it, and it's bad for you. That can make you sick." It made me proud. It made me even more delighted, but got a little awkward, when the conversation advanced further. Boy #3 says, "But why can't I have it, Daddy?" to which I replied, "Because I love you too much to let you eat things that can hurt your body. That is poison." As soon as the razor sharp, deliberately vicious word leaped from my lips with an uncanny, piercing, crystal clear pitch, I simultaneously noticed that the lady behind me was staring and listening intently. She was frozen in time, mouth breathing, with her eyes on my crew. I uncomfortably noticed that she had just handed her whining little girl the same bag of Skittles that I had just aggressively denied my offspring. Check, please!

I could go on and on about the current epidemic. How ridiculous it is that our national population is dying of malnutrition and overeating at the same time. I think this is the first time in the history of the human race that a large group of people is doing this. But hey, this is not a food book. There are plenty of other books and online resources that can teach you how to eat right and be healthy. The point of this book is just to say, in no uncertain terms, that if you are not already serious about your family's health, it's time to be. Let's just keep it simple for now. Eat lean meats. Buy ones with the least number of chemical additives and preservatives as possible. Read labels and educate yourself on what they mean. Reduce sugar intake. Eliminate fried food, even if it's a vegetable. Drink water, not cola. Consume lots of fruits, seeds, nuts, and veggies, and eat them raw when possible. Again, watch out for chemicals, dyes, pesticides, and preservatives. When in the grocery store, stick to the perimeter of the store. Stuff in bags and boxes, usually in the middle aisles that take up the most real estate, are usually not a good choice. Carbs are not evil. They are necessary for human life. But when you consume them, make sure they are whole grain and real food. These bagged and boxed items are usually the most processed with added preservatives and sugars that lack nutritional value. Lots of good things and bad things can be in the frozen section. Look carefully. Buy organic when possible. Although it will be more expensive, it's probably worth the added cost. Eliminate the junk food. It is important to splurge once in a while for psychological reasons. Once in a while, meaning like once per week. You don't have to totally surrender to everything you crave. Just remember, a cheat meal should be planned. An on-the-spot cheat meal or a repetitive one is failure and a lack of discipline. Set a day of the week to eat the forbidden temptations that you crave, but only eat them that day. Eventually, your body will adjust to the new plan and not even want the honey bun on the cheat day.

It will seem more expensive on the front end to stop buying fake food and investing in the real stuff. However, organic tomatoes are cheaper than Lipitor, Prozac, and insulin pumps later. The $14.23 you save every week buying over-processed, boxed, sugary snacks instead of fruit and granola will never compare to the price of open heart surgery in your 40's.

Remember why we started this whole conversation. It was about what is best for the baby. Your child will want you around for a while. Give him that gift. More than just adding years to your life, this new lifestyle will add energy and self-worth, which will foster a better overall family environment full of life and loaded with playful memories. All of your children will prefer that you be healthy enough to play with them. Your child will need to eat real food that is good for him, now and later. Give him that privilege. The parents are in control and have a responsibility to do this. Your household should be a healthy environment that teaches wellness, intelligence, and discipline. At some point in time, they will realize its worth and appreciate it. Don't force your children into addictive habits and lifelong struggles with bad eating habits and weight problems that are so common in our population. It all starts now. If you start well, you will likely finish well. If you put it off, it will likely never happen, and everyone will suffer for that decision. Parental neglect now will certainly compound into bigger issues later.

One more thing. If you drink too much alcohol, do something drastic. I speak from personal experience here. I was relying on wine to alleviate much of my stress for many years. I didn't realize how badly it was affecting my body until I made a change. Quit for an entire month or maybe even get some professional help. If you smoke, find a way to stop. If you are addicted to unhealthy things, find your grittiest self and fight against them. Do it for your family. These things cannot wait. They will get worse with the added burdens of active, stressful family life, especially in the early years. The time to make a dramatic and permanent change is now.

10 MONTHS BC

One Test Changes Everything

**After an excruciating day at work, two months of being *open
to the idea*, she dropped the plastic wand onto the counter as
I poured a much-needed glass of wine. It was only 5:46 p.m.
when she shouted, "Ba-bam!" The sound of the crashing
device on the countertop, the unexpected shrill sound of her
uncharacteristically piercing voice, the unmistakable look of
those two faded lines on the plastic device....I wasn't ready yet.**

So you've been working the fertility system for a while. A health
insurance plan is in place, even though you have not fully adjusted
to paying for it. You are cautiously optimistic about the future, still
doubting that you really know what you are doing. You are eating well
(or at least a lot better), feeling good, and probably realizing just how
infrequently you pooped before eating a real food diet. You have been
enjoying better quality sleep. You have an increase in energy and maybe
even an escalated sense of self-worth. You are using your newfound,
robust libido wisely and even starting to prefer the new free range
boxers over the old, snug fit briefs.

Now that there is a real chance that the newfound lifestyle and
techniques could be working, we should move on to the topic of
pregnancy testing. You need to know that testing could be exciting,

frightening, joyful, or potently disheartening. Be prepared for potential emotional fireworks in either direction. Sometimes you get both an upswing and a downswing from a single result. Life doesn't necessarily prepare you for this stuff. It's tough to know how to field your wife's emotions with this type of potential polarity. Be prepared for anything. It's impossible not to get your hopes up and become emotionally invested in the process and the results. It's the biggest thing you have ever undertaken. Nothing in your life is more important or more pivotal than the possibility of bringing a child into the world. Chances are that one of you, if not both of you, have been dreaming about this for years. Like the other significant milestones and events, you have been through in the past, you are probably nervously optimistic.

The first signs of early pregnancy are usually mild and come in the form of your wife becoming more tired and needing more sleep than usual. The lethargy may also be coupled with a sickly feeling, maybe some irritability too. For once, it's not because of you. Actually, now that I think about it, it's probably mostly because of you! These things are usually not overly dramatic in the first few weeks and can even go undetected. Women will often assume that they are a little under the weather, or simply fatigued from the stresses of everyday life. Most women first perk up and pay attention when their monthly period seems later than usual. After this goes on for a few days, she is becoming both nervous and excited in anticipation. A good guy hack here is terribly simple but revolutionary for many men. Are you ready for it? Talk to her. Ask her to keep you informed. Tell her in advance that you want to know what she's feeling and not to keep these things a secret. You need to be present with her in these times, and she will benefit from knowing that you are and will be. Guys don't typically do this, so it will be remarkable and welcomed when you propose it.

If she thinks she may be pregnant, she may prefer to see a doctor to confirm the results. The first step for most coupes is a home pregnancy test. Just like the home ovulation tests for the fertility monitor, these also require a small urine sample. A test kit can be picked up at the local pharmacy. After she puts a liquid sample on the test stick, anticipation builds. Usually, within a few long minutes, the symbols magically appear to communicate a life-altering message—pregnant or not pregnant. Most of these tests are looking for a specific hormone that is only present during pregnancy. After the sperm and egg unite, the fertilized egg must travel from its former residence in the fallopian tube to the new real estate at the uterus. Once the journey is complete, the new life form implants into the uterine wall. This implantation triggers more changes. A placenta begins to develop and hormones are released. Most pregnancy tests detect hCG (human chorionic gonadotropin), which becomes more and more measurable in blood and urine each subsequent day after implantation occurs. If it is present in urine when you test, you are almost certainly pregnant. Sometimes it can take a week or two from your successful romantic interlude before implantation takes place and the hormone level rises, which is why you don't test in the first few days immediately after the session. Some women have a sixth sense for knowing early when they are pregnant. It takes others several months to notice anything out of the ordinary and to make the connection.

Waiting five to ten minutes for the test on the bathroom counter is a nerve-racking experience that seems like an eternity. Watching those faint lines begin to appear is more suspenseful that any M. Night Shyamalan film. Many women do this part in secret and just reveal the results later. It can be a lot of fun to watch together. You both should decide ahead of time on what you prefer. Again, be prepared for crazy emotions that could swing either way. Just remain positive and available. I encourage doing these tests together so that you can offer comfort and support if the result is not what you expected.

If you get a negative result saying that she is not pregnant, you may want to test again in a few days, especially if she isn't feeling well or is still late in her usual cycle. You can usually confirm that she isn't pregnant if her period starts again. If the home pregnancy test shows that she is pregnant, you should schedule her an appointment with the OB/GYN as soon as possible. They will confirm the results with a more thorough test in the office, then immediately begin the prenatal care and baby preparation process. The doctor will likely start her on prenatal vitamins and establish a due date at this visit.

If you don't have a positive test result yet, stay the course and keep working the system. Be patient. After you get past the 12-month stage of no pregnancy, have a consult to discuss it with the doc if it may ease anxiety. Just remember that it takes most couples this long as well. You are not alone. Don't panic. A professional discussion may help everyone to relax, which is sometimes exactly what two people need for conception to work. Stress plays a key role in the fertility equation. We should reduce it whenever possible.

One more thing, when she asks if you want a boy or a girl, tell her that you just want a healthy baby and that you are insanely pumped about either possibility. Reassure her that you will rock any and all scenarios. Don't be the egotistical brat that gets hung up one way or the other and gets upset in 20 weeks when you find out that you aren't getting what you think you want. Man up and take one for the team. Don't be a jerk. This may take some maturity and some discipline. Don't make this about you. Once the baby comes, you will love either sex more than you ever thought possible. Don't add another level of stress and disappointment to the list. Be happy. Be supportive. Even if you are a little disappointed, keep it under wraps. Keep a poker face until the real joy comes. Trust me, it will.

9 MONTHS BC

Letting the Cat Out of the Bag

"Why am I getting messages from all of your family congratulating me? I haven't even told my mother yet. If she finds out on Facebook before I can talk to her, I'm going to be so mad!"

Once you have a confirmation of pregnancy, you have to decide whom to tell, how to reveal the messages, and when to go public with the news. This is not your decision. I repeat. This is not your decision. Do not tell anyone until you get explicit permission from the new mom. She probably has a priority list and wants to reveal in some methodic, possibly romantic, pre-planned sequence. Do not drop this stuff on social media until instructed to do so. Some people don't share the news right away, while some have Snapchatted the live stream before the urine has dried on the test stick. Other women may wait until they are visibly showing. Just know that you need to default to her on any breaking news reporting. One way for an emotional, hormonal grenade to detonate in your hands is for a loved one to text your wife a congratulations message before she approved the message to be delivered. She will likely want to be the one to share. If so, let her. Also, one other thing to remember: this is the biggest thing in your life, but not in everyone else's. Go easy on the public celebration. It can come across as a little narcissistic, and it also can be hard to take for people who are having a difficult time becoming pregnant. Be excited, but not obnoxious.

If there is a decision to be made on whether you both leak the info sooner or later, I would recommend sooner. This may be counterintuitive, but hear me out. It's good to have some friend and family support every step of the journey. I realize that some people wait longer out of fear because they worry about getting excited, then being devastated with a miscarriage. Some people don't want to burden others. Some want to be private with their emotions and avoid having to share sad news later. Nonetheless, I can tell you from personal experience that if something horrible happens, that's when you need the prayers and support of friends and family the most. Withholding the reports and suffering without any outside help just makes it harder on both of you. I say to share news and share the process with people that love you most. You may need them more than you think.

This topic is short and to the point. Get permission before you leak any info, and agree ahead of time whom should receive it.

Papa's Got a Brand New Identity

The new reality hasn't set in quite yet. It probably won't. Act like it has anyway.

Now that you are officially the father of an unborn child, you have to start acting like one. Now is the time to be more present than ever, physically and emotionally. There are lots of important discussions about your new life changes that must be hashed out. If she wants to talk, you talk. In case you don't already know this, a lot of time that means just listening to her talk. Most of the time, she doesn't want your words or your quick solutions. She desires your heart and needs your time and attention. Guys innately want to stop talking and just fix the problem. Women usually don't want the solution as much as they just want to discuss it… repeatedly. Provide words if prompted, but otherwise, just be available and attentive. There will be 1,000 things swirling in your head, and most likely, 200,000 in hers. Just let her know that you are still her man and that you will have her back the whole way through. Drop whatever you are doing when she has something on her mind that she wants to talk about. Let her see you cancel your plans or postpone your agenda to accommodate her needs. Keep a level head and reaffirm to her that she and your baby are your highest priority. This simple, automatic guarantee will start to lessen anxiety and help to prevent many other compounded problems that can result from stress, fear, and anxiety.

Something else that many men need to mentally prepare for is the fact that their wife's OB is about to get up close and personal on a regular basis. I say this not because I think you are unaware of the fact, but because it can be a little unsettling for some guys. Frequent exams, tests, scans, and palpations will commence over the next year. You may be surprised to know that the early sonograms require an internal component. You and your gal should talk about what visits you should attend and what is expected of you. I recommend going to as many appointments as possible. Participating in these visits allows you a chance to gain some education on what's going on, to provide moral and emotional support for your wife, and to continually strengthen your bond with your new baby. That may sound a little funny, but I'm telling you that seeing the scans, hearing the quick little heartbeats, and just appreciating the whole process makes you more in tune. There are often scary little things that have to be discussed along the way, and new moms take comfort in their man being right beside them. You may be the only guy sitting in the waiting room at the doctors' office with his lady. She will notice, and so will the staff.

Whoa! The First Trimester

Who is this woman? Who is this man? We are about to find out.

Here we go. It's time for the big show. Pregnancy is officially confirmed, and emotions are high. Everyone is feverishly planning. They call it expecting, but I don't know why. No one has any idea what to expect, especially the first time. Take a deep breath and let's set this up for success. Let's mark a few waypoints to hit on the trip and figure out the easiest route to get there before you stomp the gas pedal.

As you are probably already discovering, hormones can be super powerful... like on a nuclear level. Anything and everything in her emotions and demeanor can change in an instant, without warning. You cannot control these potent hormones, but you can provide an environment that will foster more sanity and comfort, thus preventing several common and harmful aftershocks from the inevitable, emotional explosions. You can be physically and mentally prepared for any brazen and sudden shift, and flow with it without missing a beat.

The first trimester is, in a word, crazy. It's challenging because it's so unpredictable. Pregnancy will look totally different between two women, and likely won't even be consistent between two sequential pregnancies with the same woman. The first trimester can be totally uneventful and unnoticeable, or it can be the most dramatic chaos that you have ever seen. If you find yourself googling "warning signs of spiritual possession," that would still be considered normal for a guy in your position. Sometimes it can resemble a sort of violent schizophrenia, not the sweet, blissful stroll you envisioned and hoped for. Every day can be different than the previous. Some women get sick, really sick. They can puke all morning, every day, and be fine after 1:00 p.m. Some can throw up all day long and keep it going into the late night hours. Others never get nauseous at all. Regardless of tiredness, sickness, hormonal rage, or water works from emotional instability, your role is simple: provide a hospitable environment. Protect her, defend her, and care for her. As long as you haven't given her a reason to treat you like a jerk, she won't. Well, at least not for long. Even if she has an impulsive slip-up, she will apologize and work on it, if you do your part well. In this case, the best defense is a good offense. She's working extremely hard at all levels, and the task cannot be paused or passed to someone else. Her having some time off from being pregnant is not an option. She needs to know that you are working hard yourself and noticing her efforts too. If you are doing nothing and her life is the only one requiring a dramatic change, you will likely be a victim of hormonal assault with no recourse. Affirm her. Praise her. Appreciate her. Do it often. I don't mean in a patronizing and cheesy way, and I don't mean acting like you are sincere. This is just a little reminder that you need to love her.

Everyone has different love languages and everyone shows love in different ways. Remember to love her in your way and to also love her in the way she prefers to receive it. This may mean giving her quality time together, cooking meals, giving massages, cleaning the house, working overtime hours, buying gifts, painting the nursery, giving words of affirmation, or just simply listening and being around more. In order of priority, you are now person number three. You must try to understand the gravity of the whole situation and sympathize with what she is going through, both emotionally and physically. Being pregnant and having a baby is something that she has thought about her entire life, and she is probably nervous about it. There is a lot of inherent pressure. On top of the potential fears, she's tired and in a foreign state of being because her body in doing things it has never done before. She is incubating, carrying, transporting, protecting, and feeding your baby. It is happening all day, every day, without a break.

If she feels sick, prepare her the most comfortable place to be sick. Nurse her back to sanity with Preggie Pops™, ginger ale, saltines, or any unorthodox thing you find that actually works. Clean out the trash cans, even if it's needed fifteen times per day because she blasts every can in the house with her internal eruptions. Keep the bathroom spotless if it's where she is spending 4 hours per day. Do laundry, make yourself disappear if she needs it, or build some baby furniture. I don't care if you don't know what you are doing. Just do something. Whatever works to reduce her stress is what you need to do. Furthermore, whatever works best to communicate your love and commitment, do that. For guys, something that is often exponentially harder than changing the oil in the new minivan is simply being available to talk. If she has something to say, make time to listen. Put down the phone. Better yet, let her see you power it down. If you know she is emotional or fearful, call off the plans you had previously made and be around. Talk her off the ledge and love her back to security. Reassure her and assist her. If she knows you are all in, everyone's life will be easier. Trust me.

She will likely be tired, like hit by a train tired. Allow her to rest. For gosh sakes man, she's building a human! You get tired when you have a runny nose for two days, or after you carry in the groceries. Rest is vitally important for her health and the baby's development. You know what happens when you are extremely tired. You act like an idiot, and you break stuff. Little things become big things. We must prevent this, especially during the first trimester. If she needs a nap, take over her responsibilities and give her an opportunity to do so. Even if she doesn't need one, offer her the privilege just to remind her that you are an aware and compassionate husband.

She desperately needs her rest, but healthy physical activity is also very important. Keeping in good physical shape should be a priority. Do it with her and do it for her. Pregnancy, childbirth, and recovery will all be exponentially easier if she is in good shape. Fitness is the gift that keeps on giving. Take walks, ride bikes, go to the gym, or take fitness classes together. Get in the habit now so that it becomes an automatic routine. When the baby comes, strolling as a family will be good for the soul and a wonderful addition to your routine. There are a thousand ways to get your heart pumping and your muscles working. Do something that she enjoys and something that can be maintained throughout the pregnancy, and hopefully throughout life.

There are some other key things to look out for in the first few months cohabitating with a pregnant woman. Food preferences and smells are two of them. Don't spend two hours slaving over the perfect meal without knowing ahead of time that it may be a futile gesture. I have done this numerous times, only to find that she can't bring herself to eat it. The pecan encrusted, grouper fillet with succulent asparagus, a perfect balsalmic reduction, and her favorite homemade dessert may be denied for a standard bowl of off-brand oatmeal or a handful of pickles. Smells are powerful, and you never know which ones will be good or bad. It's not just a preference for something else, the smell of something normally considered delectable can make her puke on the spot. I know what you are thinking. I'll just ask her what she wants to eat and let her pick the menu. Still dangerous, my friend! Her meal selection may seem great in her head, but once it's in the works and the sights and smells become a reality, her tastes can change in an instant. It can even happen in the four minutes it takes the taco truck to pass your meal through the window, or the fifteen minutes it takes the drone to deliver your pizza. Here's a good husband hack when it comes to food. Keep the fridge stocked with multiple healthy options at all times. Simple enough, right? Have several options at each meal and know that you may be batting cleanup to finish all the leftovers. In the times that she does have an appetite and a semi-normal sense of taste, be sure that she is getting the good stuff, not junk. If you go out on a date, let her order two things on the menu. When it arrives, you can volunteer to eat the one she prefers least.

Cravings can certainly be legit, but can also be a way for women to abuse the system and temporarily dodge the guilt. I know women who use pregnancy as an excuse to take a self-discipline vacation and not feel bad about the extended stay there. Having cravings for Rocky Road ice cream and jelly filled doughnuts every day will be a problem, like a 100-pound problem. This can lead to years of compounded issues with serious health repercussions. We see this phenomenon all too often. The added weight leads to being more tired, which leads to being more sedentary, which leads to more weight, which leads to health complications, which leads to a poor self-image, which leads to depression, which leads to marital problems, on and on. Sometimes, you may have to think rationally for the family. Wipe that sweat off your upper lip and forehead; I am not going to suggest that you rip the dripping spoon and chocolate-smattered bowl from the grips of an emotional and temporarily unstable woman with whom you must continue to cohabitate. It's easier than that. Remember when we talked about nutrition and smart eating earlier? If you do this part correctly and faithfully, the craving for junk issue will be almost nonexistent. She will crave real food instead, which is in fact what her body and the new baby need. You think a pioneer woman had cravings for Cinnabon™? Even if a craving pops up, as long as you have shopped correctly, you will only have good stuff in the house. There will be something healthy in your fridge or pantry to do the job. Keep something sweet (like watermelon), something sour (like grapefruit), and something salty (like pickles) on hand. If she demands chocolate, don't buy synthetic milk chocolate syrup full of God-knows-what. Get some real, naturally crafted chocolate made from actual cocoa. It's fine in moderation. The truth is that most cravings can be satisfied with even a small portion. I don't want you to be unsympathetic; I just want you to realize that people go way overboard with the craving thing because it's generally acceptable, and after they do, there can be a truckload of regret. Some people never recover, and those negligent choices affect them negatively forever. Remember, wellness is a lifestyle, and that lifestyle includes you.

What about alcohol and smoking? Both are a terrible idea for her and might be for you too. Both of you need to kick the smoking habit for sure. There is no definite quantity of alcohol that is safe for her to consume during pregnancy. There is also no shortage of people that will tell you that they drank during their pregnancy with no problems; but make no mistake, consuming alcohol when pregnant is always a risk. The more she drinks, the higher the risk of fetal alcohol poisoning. She may love a cold lager or a glass of merlot, but they are not worth the risk. So, what about you? If she is a lover of wine or the nightcap cocktail, be considerate. If you are sipping, swirling and moaning in intoxicated bliss during her time of alcoholic abstinence, you are just a jerk. Even if you aren't as obnoxious as I described, just openly consuming can still be annoying and painful to watch. Kudos to you if you vow to go dry for 40 weeks with her, but if you don't, just keep in mind that you are enjoying something that she cannot. As for the smoking, you know the deal. She doesn't need to smoke and neither do you. If you do, it needs to be far from her. I would encourage you to use this as your final reason and definitive time to quit. After that prized new baby that shares your DNA arrives, you will need to kick the habit anyway. You might as well start now.

If these things weren't difficult enough, here is the lemon juice on the cut: the "eating for two" mantra is a cop-out. To many people's surprise, it doesn't really take that much more food to properly nourish your growing baby. People think that they should eat twice as much at every meal since there are two people to be fed. The norm is wrong here again, and people lack the discipline to do it the right way. The world will excuse overeating during pregnancy, but that doesn't mean that it's a smart choice. Remember, the tiny person in her belly isn't a 155-pound adult. Besides, even if you need more volume, it needs to be the correct type of food. It should be nutritious food, real food, not junk. Gaining 60 pounds to have a seven-pound baby is not the right way to do it. Now she has to lose 50 pounds to feel good again, on top of being the busiest and most tired she has ever been in her life. Yeah, that sort of responsibility and stress could be trouble. You have probably seen this cascade of events negatively affect some of the people that you know. It's common but doesn't have to be. It pains me to see a woman who used to be so happy, healthy, and confident turn into a self-conscious, sometimes sad, sometimes angry person because of weight gain. It's a terrible thing that hurts women and their entire family in time. The best plan here is defense. Prevention is the key. An "I'll fix that later" attitude will not work and instead will get everyone in a difficult mess. It doesn't work with retirement planning, and it doesn't work with physical wellness. You can't easily undo the damage, so it's best to guard against it from the beginning. Unless you want a black eye, you can't tell her at 54 pounds and 30 weeks into the downward spiraling journey that it's time to cut back on the cupcakes. Talk about a toxic conversation that you will never be forgiven for mentioning. You need to have the agreement early on that BOTH of you will consume real food and get optimal nutrition and exercise. It's almost impossible to repair later.

Lucky for me, my wife is the most disciplined woman on the planet. So I have not had to coach from the sidelines too much on this one. However, I certainly accompanied her on the healthy path and did not expect her to travel it alone. Other women hate her for only gaining 10-15 pounds during pregnancy and looking like she is headed to the senior prom the week after having a baby. Her healthy condition is a result of being smart and driven, not superior genetics, as they will exclaim in a guilt-inducing diatribe. She eats good food. She eats a lot of it too, but it's the right stuff. She works out like her life depends on it, and I am right by her side doing it too. She does not compromise or make excuses, and she is validated in the hard work by knowing that she is doing it for the whole family. Nonetheless, the other women have a hard time liking her for it. They give her the, "That must be nice" response instead of asking her to teach them the way. By the time they realize it is their fault, it's too late. Just hear me on this. Do not be surprised at the passive aggressive comments from friends and complete strangers.

So many women will still be trying to lose 32 pounds of "baby weight" a year later, and their husband will have put on an additional 20 himself. Often, when my wife meets another woman for the first time, they will ask how old her baby is. She will say that of her four, the youngest is two months. Then they will say something like, "I can't stand you," in a joking way, absolutely meaning it the whole time. The truth is that no one will dare bring up that there is a difference between *baby weight* and *bonbon weight*. One woman asked my wife recently, "What's the secret to losing the baby weight so fast?" Before she could respond to the disgruntled, insincere, but smiling woman, I responded, saying, "You have a baby." Later, after my wife scolded me and informed me that I was being rude and shouldn't have said that, I realized that she was right. I should have included the placenta, water breakage, and a good bowel movement to have been totally honest and more accurate response to the question. Those things account for at least a few more pounds.

This may all seem a little harsh and rude to some, but let's remember two related realities on this subject. A healthy baby depends solely on a healthy mother, and a mother should not have to do it alone. The entire household needs to be healthy. It's probably true that many healthy babies are born to women who eat nothing but ice cream. It's also true that many women get into a state of insecurity and self-hate after pregnancy because they can never reel it back in. That's not healthy for anyone in the family.

So make a commitment to shop smart, to eat smart, and not to cheat. Everyone is on the same plan. Stay off the junk, the cigarettes, drugs, or anything else that is detrimental to optimal health, and keep moving. All three of you will be better for it for your entire lives.

The Worst Day of Her Life

A few words on miscarriage

As much as I despise this subject, we must take a detour to discuss it before getting into the second trimester. Miscarriage is something that very few people willingly talk about. Much like the infertility issues we talked about earlier, we assume that it's rare because we don't hear about it too much. The fact is that it's extremely common for women to have a miscarriage in the first trimester. Some statistics say that one in five pregnancies ends this way.

My wife and I have been through this dreadful event two times in our parental journey together. Both times were in the first trimester, which is the most common time for a miscarriage. My youngest sister-in-law had a miscarriage in the first trimester too, and my oldest sister-in-law lost a child just before her due date. These experiences are insanely painful and can wreak havoc on emotions, confidence, and relationships.

I will speak only about my direct experience losing two of my children. It is horrible. One time was tough. Two times was brutal. You immediately crash from very high to very low. It's disheartening and very emotional. Your wife does not heal quickly, and there are lasting effects from it. Most guys have trouble understanding this. I have watched from the sidelines as my peers go through it, the woman dying inside, and the man going on about his business, pretending it never happened. Most men have no idea what they should be doing, so they retreat. They sprint back to their normal life as soon as possible to escape the foreign and uncomfortable atmosphere that miscarriage created. This withdrawal from him makes it worse on her. So many guys leave her to suffer alone, and she quietly does just that. Fathers will never be able to understand what losing a child inside of their body is like. To be safe, assume that it's just like losing a close friend. Even though they have never met, mothers have loved that child instinctively, in a profound way. Suffer with her and be present. Do not abandon her.

Perhaps, the best way to present this is to allow you to peer into my heart by way of a memoir that I wrote a few days after our first miscarriage. This was written by a desperate man. I was in a manic, confused, unprepared, fearful, and sad place. I was watching my wife suffer and trying to be present to her needs, all the while my heart was also in pieces. I was blindsided and had never even thought about this as a possibility before. I had no instruction manual or guiding mentor for this hardship. I knew she needed me to be something, but I wasn't sure whom or how. I don't know where you stand on God and creation, but I make no apologies for where I stand. You will probably see exactly where when you read this. You may have a different coping mechanism, but this view of God helped me, and us, get through it. I wrote these exact words many years ago, a few days after our first miscarriage. I hope it's helpful to you. It may also be beneficial to someone that you know is suffering in the same way.

Here it is:

"The prefix *mis* is meant for negative use to mean bad or badly—as in misinterpret, mispronounce, or mistake. The word *miscarriage* would simply mean a bad carrying of something, in this particular case, carrying of a soul and a chosen child of God. On matters of creation, the word miscarriage is an oxymoron, and I find it completely offensive. The eternal Father, the creator of the universe and all that is Holy, planned this precious soul and knew this child even before conception. There has been no mistake, and most certainly, no poor carrying.

She and I were chosen to co-create with our Father to bring this child into the world. There needed to be a human vessel, or this soul would never have been created for the Kingdom of God. I consider it an honor that we have been chosen for this task. We have been blessed with a healthy son before this child, and I am so unbelievably grateful for him. I have been squeezing him much tighter this week. But whether this recent child had been lost at six weeks in utero or had outlived both parents, God looks at him or her the same in either case: as a daughter, a son, a precious soul.

I have never experienced pain of this level in my personal life. However, I am not angry with God. To be very honest, I am personally surprised by this realization. I know that if I could see His face, He would have even more tears than I have right now. I realize that it would only be selfish to be angry. If I am asked to bear an open wound, that is the least of what I can do in exchange for the gift of security in knowing a sovereign God. I have heard on many occasions that we are to bear our cross and carry it daily. I am starting to understand at least a fraction of what this means now. I never even felt like I had anything heavy enough to merit being called a cross before. In some unexplainable way, this experience has led me closer to the Father, not just because I hurt and I am in real need of help right now, but because I feel like I understand Him a little better as The Father. As we found out that there were complications with this pregnancy, our prayers remained the same. Our prayer was for God's will to be done and for the grace, wisdom, and strength to accept this will. Our desire was for a healthy, full-term baby. God knew our desire but answered our prayer. I am inconsistent in most everything in my life; I am, however, very consistent in at least one task—I pray for peace for my family every day. I am coming to a better understanding of what peace actually is now.

Peace is not a lack of suffering. Peace is being able to suffer without fear. I think that peace explained in a simple word would be freedom. At the present time, being able to suffer in peace is an outpouring of God's grace. It is a gift. I am so grateful for this extra grace and even more grateful that the same grace has been given to my wife - undoubtedly much more than to me. Words are unable to describe the respect and admiration that I have for her right now. I cannot pretend to understand what it is like to be the carrier of such a precious soul. No one knows a child as a mother does. I know that my prayer for peace has been answered in a profound way. I thank God for such a tremendous gift in such a fragile and needy time.

We are taught to store up treasures in heaven. I think that I am beginning to understand at least part of what this means now. I hope for the day that I get to meet this precious child of God personally. I cannot wait to embrace and express my love and gratitude for him or her. I usually stay away from talk of people being in heaven and thoughts of what it must be like up there. However, right now I cannot stop thinking of all the children that must be there. From what I read, one in five pregnancies ends early. That adds up to an amazing number of souls. I guess God needs these for reasons beyond my comprehension. I know as much as He loves these children, it must be a wonderful place to be. I also take comfort in thinking of my family members that have left us and how cool it is that they are welcoming this new child into a new realm of existence.

The prefix *mit* means to send, as in the words *transmit* and *remit*. This is the prefix that should be used for the carrying and then sending a child to be with the Father. This mit-carriage has impacted me in ways beyond words. I know this journey will continue. This child has ministered to me in this mystery, and I am forever grateful for that. I will miss this child every day of my life on Earth, but I take pride in the job that was chosen for us. I will continue to suffer in peace, but if asked to carry on this mission again, I will say, "Yes, Lord, may your will be done in my life, and somehow may my life here add glory to your Kingdom. Amen."

If this tragedy happens to you, you and your wife need to take some time off. You need time to grieve. This is a loss that only someone who has been through it can relate to. You cannot just go on, business as usual, as if nothing happened, and expect to function normally. A real problem with miscarriage is that the world doesn't have an official, accepted protocol on this. When a person dies that has made it outside of the womb, there are social norms. There are ceremonies, visitations, meals, and most certainly time off from work and other obligations. When your unborn child dies, there should be something in place to help you cope. The family should gather together for support. You should have some time off and maybe even some sort of ceremony. We did. We didn't publish it in the paper and invite the world. We just asked a few family members to join us in offering prayers and to support us in our period of grieving. Just being together and supporting each other helped us all. Many years later, I still grieve those babies, and so does my wife. I'm especially reminded of them when I see parents with a child that they apparently don't want. This is painful to see, and it's almost impossible for me not to be angry with them. Here we are trying to have children, wanting to care for them, and others are having them repeatedly, wanting nothing to do with them, and taking it all for granted. This is real life, and often times, real life is unfair.

I must say that we learned what vulnerability really feels like after accepting the responsibility of trying to get pregnant again. We were both gun-shy after the first miscarriage. When the next pregnancy ended the same way, we were very wounded and began to worry. After being beaten up twice, accepting another try was extremely difficult. We had to muster up some real courage and put our feelings and fears on the line. We did, and it paid off in the form of multiple wonderful boys. The easier path would have been to protect our emotions and just stop trying. The right path was to band together and rely on each other. We both wanted more children and could not deny it. It was a time of growth and dependency on each other and ended up strengthening us as individuals and as a couple. For some, the marriage doesn't finish in a better place. It takes everything you've got to come out with your head above water. It's much better to have your friends and family support you and cut you some slack. Don't keep it a secret and carry it all alone.

What's next? Well, friend, you must use your best judgement to gauge the tempo for when to move forward. With that said, my recommendation is to be present, talk, pray, take time to heal, and eventually, to try again. Trying again will take courage and vulnerability, but I can tell you with certainty that the best source of healing will likely be to band together and to offer all of yourselves for something potentially greater. It goes without saying that it will certainly be a celebrated and joyful moment if you do find that desired child in your arms one day.

6 MONTHS BC

Whew! The Second Trimester

Wait… Is that sunshine piercing through the dark clouds? I think the storm is over. Hey, you're back! Babe, it's really great to see you again.

The second trimester is usually fun. The puke-a-thon is over. Hormones have equalized, and your wife is starting to get her normal personality and temperament back. You will get to see a new ultrasound image that more closely resembles a person and not a kidney bean. That's cool! If you choose to, you get to find out the sex of the child you are obsessing about, which is amazing. You're cruising now. Everyone is happy for your new family, and you think you are getting more mentally prepared too. Instead of managing foreign feelings, the second trimester is usually about getting prepared and feeling excited.

At around 20 weeks, it will be time for a sonogram, although some doctors will allow it a few weeks earlier. Just know that you can't tell too much from the scan concerning the child's sex if it's much earlier than 20 weeks. Try to be patient. At this appointment, the sonogram will be external, with a handheld unit that scans on little Momma's stomach. These units are much better than the internal unit used before that looked like Bob Barker's old microphone from *The Price is Right*. It's more comfortable, and since pants stay on, visitors can come in to see too. This visit is more than just checking for anatomy that will hopefully confirm gender if you elect to find out. They will measure your little one's body parts and check growth milestones. This is all done digitally and is really cool stuff. You can get prints of the scans, or get them on a CD or jump drive to take home.

You probably already know about the 4D optional sonograms. Most people do this just to see a better picture of their little developing family member. It's kind of like a picture, but more like a Play-Doh™ 3D rendering of a child-like object that hasn't been totally finished yet. Sometimes the images aren't the best quality on this visit, and after the expense is paid, it can be a letdown. I've never seen anyone obtain images that look like the ones on the brochure. It's totally a matter of preference, but know that results do vary. It can be an expensive luxury that ends in disappointment if a quality image isn't captured or if the baby isn't in an ideal position for a photo op. You can decide what it's worth to you and if you want to add this extra scan. It's exciting to finally find out what's in there. Now you can say "he" or "she" instead of "it." You can start to more clearly imagine what you think life will be like in the coming years. If you have already chosen a name, you can begin to use it immediately. I support the idea of naming early so you can talk to him and allow him to hear your voice speaking his name. If you don't think talking to him for six months matters, you are mistaken. They will learn your voice and respond better and faster once they make it to the other side. Start talking to your child, even if it feels strange at first. You will most likely find that the bizarre practice of speaking into a woman's belly button will have a positive emotional effect on Mom too. It's sweet and shows a level of commitment and sincerity.

I want to throw something else in here because a shameful habit is commonplace in many modern relationships, and I think it shouldn't be. It's a tragedy that causes everyone in the home to suffer. That habit is yelling at each other. If you are a high volume, argumentative type of guy, this would be a good time to learn to stop doing it in the house. Work on those bad tendencies to fight with your spouse. You should have quit that a long time ago anyway, right? After all, fighting is selfish 98% of the time. Speaking to your wife in the same tone you use to scold a dog is disrespectful and most definitely a result of a lack of self-control. You want your baby to be in a peaceful environment. You don't want him to learn bad habits from you in the future, and you want to have a better relationship with your wife. Those are three worthy reasons to improve. Simple enough. We also want to set the right example for our children as they mature and learn from our example. If this hits close to home, maybe it's time to work on it. I encourage you to do just that. You may find this hard to believe, but I'm going to share it. I never heard my father yell at my mother. Never! It wasn't that he was a doormat, a pushover, or that he always agreed. He just made a decision long ago, after being hurt by his father's anger, to stop the madness. He never had to verbally instruct me on how to respect a woman, he showed me. My wife will gratefully and happily tell you that she has never received verbal assault or screaming from me. I give total credit to my dad. He trained me for success. He hacked my marriage by pre-conditioning me to have self-control, to be respectful, and to work things out in a non-hostile way. I hope my kids pick it up from me, and I hope yours pick it up from you. It's powerful stuff and a tremendous gift. I'll get off that soapbox now, and we'll trudge on. Now we can focus on some fun stuff.

The Name Game

So what about the name? Some couples are totally prepared, having both a girl and a boy name picked out months in advance, waiting for the verdict to come in. Sometimes the deliberation over a name, or over multiple names, can last all 40 weeks. I know a few parents that hadn't decided until after the child was breathing room oxygen in the hospital nursery. Don't get bent out of shape if you cannot agree on a name immediately. One name that you have always loved will be one that she hates. Your favorite may be the name of the crazy pervert that dated her best friend. The one she has always liked happens to be the name of the creepy kid that used to shoot spitballs and pick his nose beside you in 4th grade. The good thing is that there are millions of options out there. Keep making lists privately, then come together to review them with each other. Go through family histories, baby naming books, and maybe do some name trending research online. It's fun to go through your lists together. You may not come to a 100% agreement, but you will find some common ground. This is one of the rare times that I will not just encourage you to let her have her way to keep the peace. A name is very important, and you should reach an agreement on this issue. Don't be belligerent about it, but be patient and wait until you find an agreeable match. Sometimes you need to marinate for a few weeks on a name to get a good feel. Be patient and compassionate.

Consider one more hack when playing the name game. You may want to withhold your preferred names from friends and family until it's officially decided. I highly recommend maintaining a tight-lipped practice until the end of the naming process. Sometimes people will share their opinion too openly and hurt your feelings. If your mother-in-law says that she hates a name you are heavily considering, it really can be a buzzkill. It's not her decision or anyone else's. Wait until you are sure of it. Don't ask for outside opinions on the top contenders. Simply announce the final name once you and the Mrs. have definitively decided.

Where and How to Have a Baby

Does anybody know where to buy an inflatable kiddie pool in January? How do we get the garden hose unfrozen?

Two more critical things that should be determined by this point are: where to have the baby, and how to have the baby. Let's start with the *where* question. You know that there is a growing trend of people having babies at home. Many people are using a doula or a midwife instead of an OB/GYN. Some people go this route because of the potential cost savings. Others like this option because they are concerned with being in a germ-infested hospital. There are also the all-natural, holistic types, who want to do it the natural, old-fashioned way. They choose to deliver in their bathtub, in their bedroom, in a kiddie pool in the living room, or on an organic, hand-woven, hemp hammock in a free-range chicken coop. You do whatever you think is best, but don't choose an option to be cool or to have an amazing Facebook™ video to share. Choose it because you think it's the best option for your family. I have seen first-hand what it looks like when there are complications during labor. Personally, I don't want to be anywhere that doesn't have all the necessary equipment in case of trouble. We have been, and most likely will continue to be, delivering in a hospital every time. Hastily searching through my kitchen drawer for salad tongs, while my wife is screaming in the living room, just before passing out, is not my idea of a good time. I do not mean to make light of this subject or to insult anyone. Choosing a birthing location is a significant decision that carries lots of emotional weight.

I'm sure that when everything goes smoothly, home birth is beautiful. However, bad things can happen, and those things scare me to death. Complications are more common with first-time deliveries. There may be problems with Mom, with the baby, and even with Dad. Sometimes, one of the parties needs to go to the OR, ICU, or NICU. Sometimes they need to get on a helicopter and speed to another facility for emergency attention. There may be the need for some cutting, some suction, or some IV drugs to get that baby that is suffering trauma out faster. You don't get a trophy for doing it at home. If something goes wrong at home, you will likely blame yourself for that decision and never get over it. My personal recommendation is to plan on delivering at the hospital because it's the safest place to be if things go awry. I know that the hospital has a lot of unwanted diseases and germs within its walls, but hopefully that is all on a different floor or in a different building and has been properly addressed. You can do the research yourself and make some informed decisions. I am not passing judgment on home birth parents. I just want you to consider all the options and make a decision on what's best for your family. Plan and hope for the best, but be prepared for the worst.

So now you know that I like to deliver at the hospital. We do use a midwife there. Why? Because our midwife is awesome. Her care and bedside manner are superior to the docs in the practice. She is very capable, and my wife loves her.

The other item after the *where* is the *how*. There are many locations, positions, and methods to discuss with your doctor or midwife. But beyond these is a more important question. That is whether or not to use medicine. Specifically, I mean induction meds and epidurals. Pitocin™ is the most common IV drug used to speed up labor. It's a synthetic form of oxytocin, which is a hormone that causes labor. Slowly introducing this drug with IV fluids causes more frequent and stronger contractions and speeds dilation. There is a lot of pressure to do this by many doctors and hospitals. Many clinics prefer this method because it makes scheduling easier and more predictable for them. They want to make a schedule ahead of time and have everyone on it and ready to go. Scheduling inductions means that the on-call doc may not have to be bothered to get out of bed and come to the hospital at 3 a.m. It also means that the hospital can stack more people onto the schedule, making more money. They can also generate a few more services and fees to add to your bill. You may think it's a good idea too so that you can plan your schedule. The problem is that your wife isn't getting her teeth cleaned, she's having a baby! It's a huge process with nine months' worth of natural, chain reactions that lead up to one giant crescendo. There are about 10,000 events in the child development sequence that need to be in place before labor and delivery begin. It's an amazingly complex process. Some healthy women naturally deliver babies at 38 weeks. Others will routinely go two or three weeks past their due dates before going into labor. Timing is a large part of it. Inducing labor does increase the chances of needing a C-section and can increase the risk of other complications, both during delivery and after. Sometimes, the situation is started prematurely, and things progress at the wrong pace. For this reason, my wife and I do not do planned inductions unless medically necessary. If your wife is a small person or it's her first time delivering, the medical staff may not want her to go past her due date and may recommend inducing labor before that day. If there are early problems with the baby or Mom, the doctor may decide that an induction is necessary. There are certainly special circumstances that would make inducing labor the best decision. Do it out of necessity, not convenience. Again, there are tons of articles to check out on this topic. Do some informed research on it so that you can make the healthiest decision. Always discuss these things with your doctors.

So, you heard it correctly; I am not a fan of scheduled inductions for mere convenience. I think a woman should go into labor naturally as long as everything else is going well and the baby is safe. That is unless she is well beyond her due date or begins to have complications. Modern medicine is well equipped to take care of premature babies. Sometimes it is a very smart idea to get them out early when there is evident trouble inside. Please don't plan to induce a week early because you want to make it to a birthday party the week after. Everything else can take a back seat to this event. Nothing is more important.

The other question on the drug topic is whether or not to get an epidural. This is a procedure that is usually administered by an anesthesiologist or nurse anesthetist. A test dose of the potent medicine will be delivered at a specific nerve location in her back. The fluid goes into the epidural space around her spine. The goal of an epidural is to provide analgesia, or pain relief, rather than anesthesia, which leads to total lack of feeling. Sometimes you get both, and everything below the waist gets numb. But if completed with ideal results, the Mrs. will be able to move her legs but not feel pain in the lower half of her body, most notably in the pelvis area where the monster pain is going to be unleashed. A test dose is given to confirm the location and monitor for any potential allergy or other adverse reaction. Once the test is successful, a small tube, or catheter, is inserted that will deliver medicine consistently to the spot. The delivery of medication is usually controlled by some form of an electronic pump. The benefit here is obvious: no pain!

You know as well as I do that many women want to go all-natural and give birth without any relief from an epidural. Again, I don't want to sound condescending, and I will let you all work this out on your own. I don't have a dog in your fight on this, and what I am going to say may surprise you. However, I must ask those people who insist on doing it drugless, "Are you freaking crazy?" There is no trophy for this. You don't get inducted into the Mother's Hall of Fame for screaming in pain, biting pillows, and eventually pulling it off after spewing expletives and insulting everyone in the Labor & Delivery wing. Are you surprised at my tone? We do eat a strictly all-natural diet at my house, but we also appreciate the advances of modern medicine. Maybe we could be considered hypocrites, but if we have an infection, we might take some antibiotics. If we have a headache, we may take a Tylenol™ or an ibuprofen. If we are having a baby, you bet your wallet that we get an epidural!

I know that some people are naturalists, hippies, or whatever else you want to call it, and if that's your wife and she wants to tough it out, go for it. If you are doing it just for bragging rights, but not for some deep maternal connection or health reasons, you may want to think about it again. There is one vital issue to understand that gets a lot of people in trouble. A lot of women will say that they want to skip the meds, and these same people will adamantly change their position when they hit about 9 centimeters in the delivery room, just before it's time to start pushing. The caveat here is that there is a point where you cannot change your mind. The specialist cannot insert the catheter on a woman during active contractions. Your bride may not be able even to sit up by the time she waves the white flag. In this case, she will be denied the help, and there is no choice but to suffer along and finish without it. Many, many women change their mind at 5 centimeters, and many more try to go back on the decision at 8, 9, or 10. The pain can be inconceivable and unbearable. It is unlike anything she has ever felt, and the initial decision was unfortunately based on her previous pain experiences. Her prior pain scale is relative. Her previous 10 may actually only be a 5.75 on the newfound, childbirth-enlightened pain scale. So if you are going for it, just know that it's going to be tough. Some women say, "I want to try it," assuming that the back-out plan is an option. A half-committed approach to test the situation is a bad idea. In the words of Yoda the Jedi, "Do or do not, there is no try." If she wants to tough it out so that she can tell the child that she did so one day, so be it. However, appreciate that a horrible experience could affect your chances of doing this whole baby thing again in the future. Hopefully, the natural, post-delivery hormones that induce amnesia for mothers will do their job. Nonetheless, if there are legitimate health reasons for abstaining from drugs, I understand. I'm just being honest on this because I think many people won't.

I have never seen a woman give birth naturally, so I cannot speak first-hand. But several of my buddies and their wives say that they hope to never experience it again. The first baby is almost always the hardest to deliver and takes the longest to come through the birth canal. If she is thinking about childbirth without any anesthesia, it may be beneficial to try to convince her to consider doing that on baby number two or three, and maybe play it safe and painless on the first. Don't have a fight about it, but at least discuss the pros and cons. It's her decision in the end. Do not, I repeat, do not pressure her to go all natural so you can brag about it. This is her decision. Just remember, if she does go all natural, don't take it personal when she tells you what she thinks of you and your mother in the heat of battle.

The final element that must be worked out is what types of film and pictures you want during the delivery process. You need to talk about it way ahead of time so that you have what you need, and you can add it to your checklist. We always elected to film the delivery and to position the camera, so it shows Mommy's point-of-view. This camera angle serves two functions: she can remember it the way it happened and reflect on what she saw on that remarkable day, and if she ever wants to share the footage, friends and family aren't staring at her highly personal parts. If you want still pics and video, you will need an accomplice so that you don't end up with both hands occupied, capturing poor screen shots on both fumbling devices, and not having a hand for your wife to hold. I recommend recruiting her mother or significantly close friend or family member to be in charge of one device. Oh, and just in case you were thinking of doing so, don't pin it, post it, update it, or share it until much later with her explicit permission. Be in the moment and watch it first-hand. The rest of the world can wait.

3 MONTHS BC

Ugh! The Third Trimester

Geez, will 39 weeks ever get here? The happy trimester has expired and now the clock is ticking much louder... or is that a gong? Six months in seems like it's been so long, but there is still a ways to go.

Every passing week gets more and more uncomfortable for the expectant mom. She has less room inside for basic necessities, like a bladder. She has to go more often, and it has to happen around the clock. It's harder and harder for her to get comfortable. She's working harder, getting hotter, and running out of gas earlier every day. She needs more rest, probably even more than the first trimester. It's now difficult to lie flat or to find a good sleeping position for more than a few hours. Lots of tossing and turning is to be expected.

Many times in the third trimester, mothers will begin to have labor-like symptoms early. These typically happen toward the end of the trimester but can show up several months earlier. The early pains and rumblings may be the mild, non-labor contractions called Braxton Hicks contractions. They are very common. In contrast to a labor contraction, this type can become more comfortable with a change in position. These aren't as painful as the real thing, but they can be concerning to Mom, especially if she has never felt any contractions before. They can even happen on a regular schedule and create some premature excitement. It's not considered early labor unless there is continuous strengthening in the intensity of the contractions, and they are accompanied by dilation and effacement. Dilation and effacement can also start several weeks (even months) early. Sudden changes could be totally normal and not a big deal, or could be very alarming and serious. Always inform her doctor of any new developments.

Effacement is the process by which the cervix starts to prepare for delivery. Once the baby drops low enough into the pelvis, he gets closer to the cervix and causes a fascinating chain reaction. The cervix will begin to stretch and become softer, shorter, and thinner. It's also sometimes called ripening or cervical thinning. These changes cause hormonal changes and muscle changes that cause more contractions. During a healthy pregnancy, the cervix has been closed and is covered by a protective coating, or plug, made of thick mucus. As effacement happens, the plug gets more and more loose and eventually is dislodged and passes. This passing of the plug is sometimes called a bloody show because it normally passes with some blood. It may happen in the delivery room or several hours before you arrive there. Sometimes it's very small and never even noticed. You will hear effacement referred to as a percentage and usually follows a dilation measurement. The doctor or nurse will say, "She is 2 centimeters dilated and 40% effaced." When she is 10 centimeters dilated and 100% effaced, it's time to have a baby. These numbers will be checked several times in the third trimester and many times on D-day.

After the cervix begins to efface, it will also begin to open, which is called dilation. Cervical dilatation is monitored by repeatedly checking with a gloved finger to feel the width of the opening. The diameter of the opening is measured in centimeters. Zero means that the cervix is totally closed, and 10 means that it is fully dilated. Ten centimeters is about 4 inches. Her cervix must be completely dilated before starting to push. Sometimes a woman can be slightly dilated for weeks or more before the baby comes. A few centimeters open can be common late in the pregnancy, even if she is not in labor. If the dilation becomes too exaggerated, too early, the doctor may intervene. If the baby drops into the low pelvic position too early, the pressure triggers all the other sequences in the chain reaction to move faster. Sometimes, women will dilate or begin to efface weeks, or even months, early. Some women do this with every pregnancy, make it full term, and never have a problem. In some cases, though, it may be more serious, and the reactions should be slowed. Bed rest, exercises, positioning, or medication may be needed to halt the laboring process. Your OB will let you know if any changes are necessary. Just know that in the case that lowering activity is necessary, or bed rest is warranted, you will need to step up and once again, be prepared to work harder as the man of the house. Just follow directions, and lean to the side of caution. Early babies usually mean added stress, concerns, and expenses. Don't let her overdo it. You are the protector of both of them. It's your job.

Let's hustle on to the rest of the prep that needs to commence during this trimester for most every case. Much like the plan for the first trimester, the strategy is simple. That is, to make her as comfortable as possible. In the first trimester, discomfort was more a result of hormonal chaos. In the last trimester, discomfort is more attributed to physically being a larger person with a more demanding load. If she wants to be in pajamas and maintain a home temperature preferable to a polar bear, that's okay. Grant her that luxury. She's working hard and getting zero breaks. Dress however necessary to avoid becoming a burden to her. Don't complain about the temperature, her bathroom frequency, or her flip-flops. Let her know you are on her team. If she needs the side of the bed closest to the bathroom, give it up. If she requests sleeping in another bed altogether, cater to her the request. It may actually be a big help for you. Just make sure it was her idea.

The other thing that must happen during this final incubator phase is hospital prep. You must prepare emotionally, physically, and logistically. First, let's talk about logistics. One thing you want to do sooner than later is to pre-register at the hospital. It's best for the expectant mother to register weeks before she needs any services. Presenting all of the patient information and insurance details will save a few steps later when you are in a mad rush to have a baby.

It doesn't matter if your wife is having paranoid, fake labor or about to birth a child on the ER waiting room floor, no one at the hospital will be in a rush when you arrive. The hospital staff deals with false alarms all the time. Many people come in too early and are monitored for a few hours and subsequently sent back home. Common false alarms have created a "boy who cried wolf" phenomenon. Even if you have never had a false alarm, the staff still assumes that you are having one because of how many they see every month.

The hospital's lack of urgency is particularly present with your first baby. They will ask, "Is this your first?" If you are not an honest person, or if you believe in conditional dishonesty, this would be the time to lie. You will be taken more seriously if they think you aren't a rookie. OK, I can't encourage you to fib. Maybe you can be honest and just be more creative. When they say, "Is this your first?" you can give a confident look and say, "It's my first with her." (ATTENTION: Be sure you discuss this comment ahead of time with your wife if you plan to use it.) Hey, cut me some slack. It's true, and it is a great hospital triage hack. If and when your wife is in real, active labor, it starts to get really painful. Nothing will tick you off quite like a nonchalant, somewhat bitter, condescending hospital worker belittling your wife's emergent state. Fifteen minutes of paperwork can feel like an eternity, but if you have pre-registered, you can skip some of this frustrating drama. They will need information about her insurance, referring doctor, medical history, etc. The front office will likely request quite a bit of personal data concerning you too.

Here's the luxury hack that you never expected. When you call to pre-register, ask them about L&D room options. Most people are unaware, but some hospitals and birthing centers take room reservations just like the Ritz Carlton. There are a limited number of suites at some hospitals, and they are often first come, first served (or at least first paid, first reserved.) Our first childbirth was in a small hospital that had about 14 rooms, some of which were singles, and some were shared. They also had two additional, oversized suites. I paid extra in advance (I think it was like 200 bucks) to lock down one of these primo spots. The place was glorious. We had a mini-fridge, a microwave, a sofa, a small separate visiting area, and even a fold out bed for Dad. Jackpot! A deluxe room is likely not available everywhere, but don't miss out because you neglected to ask.

Specify that you would like a private room, even if there is no other upgrade. Tell them your wife is going all natural with no anesthesia. Then let them know that she screams at an amazing pitch, cusses like a drunken sailor, and has a tendency to throw things when under stress. Do whatever you have to do to get a private room. OK, don't lie about that either, but close the sale in whatever way you can. You may have to deliver cookies and be extremely polite to the gatekeeper at the hospital a few weeks in advance. Seriously though, even if everything is super smooth, you do not want to share this experience with total strangers, especially when they are four feet away behind a thin, 80's inspired, pastel curtain. Request a private room, and ask for the most spacious one. It never hurts to ask.

Once you are registered and have the VIP lounge on lock, you need to lay out an action plan to get there when the code red is activated; I mean, when she starts active labor. It's good to have an L&D bag packed for the last month or two of the pregnancy. Most first-timers will make it to full term (at least 38 weeks), but it's certainly common to start laboring a week or two before the due date. Many women have early contractions that do not lead to labor. These alarming events may create a false-alarm visit or two. However, don't be selfish! If your wife is having contractions and wants to go to the hospital to get monitored, go. Even if it's 3:30 a.m., go. There is too much at stake not to check it out. One of my best buddies, Chuck, delivered his second baby girl (he's not an OB/GYN) in the front seat of his car, in the hospital parking lot, because they didn't make it in time. The automobile birth didn't result from negligence or ignorance; everything just progressed very quickly. As cool as this may sound to receive such an accolade, it's not a good plan for you, Mom, or the new baby. I told my man Chuck that I thought it was awesome for three reasons: He had just been inducted into a new level of manhood that very few men will ever achieve. He now had an amazing story and a unique bond with his daughter that will live forever. I think he saved like $9,000 in delivery fees. He quickly and emphatically informed me that he didn't recommend trying it that way, that he never wanted to do it again, and the surprisingly menial discount was nowhere near worth it. I still thought he was a rock star, for whatever that's worth. Regardless, the take-home lesson is to err on the safe side and always be ready to go. Just know that real labor contractions are usually pretty painful and can escalate rapidly.

So, what's in the to-go bag that you keep ready? There are two separate collections that you need to assemble. One is a "comfort" bag; the other is a "save you some serious dough" bag. For the "comfort" bag, just think of all the essentials you and the Mrs. will need. Treat it like a three-day stay in a lousy motel with bad food, no rest, and constant interruptions. Hey, at least room service is one button away at all times. You need clothes, toiletries, and all the normal stuff. It's also wise to take pillows and blankets for yourself. They likely won't have a bed for you, even though you will be there for a few nights. Hospital floors are nasty, so some cheap (possibly throw-away) slippers are a good idea. Small bills for late night vending machines are good to have. Don't forget chargers and electronics. Some form of entertainment is nice too. Magazines, tablets, laptop, books, snacks, and a few water bottles are always beneficial to have on hand.

Now for a few things that you probably haven't thought about. These two paragraphs will pay for this book and the thank you card that you will send me, including priority postage. This hack is also known as the "save you some serious dough" bag. At the hospital, they charge you ridiculous amounts of money for EVERYTHING. If you open a $1 mini-box of Kleenex™, they probably call it sanitation fabric and charge you $78 for it. A few things she will need, but you do not want on your hospital bill, include socks, a thermos (for drinking), a squeezable/squirt-able water bottle (for rinsing the southern hemisphere), baby diapers, and wait for it… adult diapers. Ok, maybe not technically adult diapers, but huge feminine pads and some oversized, cheap undies. I know this is foreign to you, but get your wife to ask another mom about it. After delivery, she must wear the pad, often with ice in it, in a stretchable pair of mesh underwear. She must also rinse a few times per day with the squirt bottle. On our last visit, they filled a baby diaper with ice and made that the ice pack. They probably billed us for "thermodynamic compression dressing" and charged $287 for it. You can pick this stuff up for $20 and save $500.

The next little gem that you need to know about is the so-called "self-medication pack." The package is a triad of simple pills that will be given after delivery. The medicinal cocktail consists of acetaminophen (Tylenol™), ibuprofen (Advil™), and Colace™. These are all available without a prescription in any drug store. Acetaminophen is for pain, ibuprofen is for inflammation, and the final one is a stool softener. If the hospital gives you these three things to take yourself during recovery, it will cost you about $300. If you pick them up at the local pharmacy, they cost about $8. If you have all the supplies yourself, you save a bunch of money. My wife always tells each nurse as they enter the room for the first time, "Don't give us anything that is optional. Don't open any packages of anything without telling me. I'm not trying to be rude or pushy, just trying to save some money." They usually laugh and then cooperate, saving us anywhere from $500-$2,000 over a three-day period. In the end, the nurses all appreciate the extra effort we make. They almost always dismiss us with a bag full of freebies and samples to take home. One time we received an entire pad of baby formula and diaper vouchers worth about $600. Some even bigger, bottom-line savers will come in a few chapters. I will remind you about this later once you get to the big show.

Another ingredient for a seamless labor transition is a travel plan with a backup route. Know the fastest way to get to the hospital and a secondary plan in case of traffic. It's also beneficial to go ahead and make a call list of important people that need to know what's going on when the big day arrives. If the expectant mother is whisked away to surgery in an instant, you need to have already discussed the contact plan and have the necessary info tucked away. You need to know who needs to know, and how to reach them. Group texts are convenient but can get out of hand rapidly. One great hack is to get a friend to run quarterback for you on messaging. Give a close friend or family member the contact list, and just send her updates so that she can relay the info to everyone. That way, no one gets upset with you "missing moments" because you are on your phone, and no one on the list gets accidentally left out in all the pandemonium. If they do get left out, you can blame someone else. You were busy. Again, don't send messages or put anything on social media unless your wife explicitly approves of it first. She's about to be deranged and emotional, and you don't need any ammunition for the crazy cannon that may be smoking in a few hours, days, or weeks.

If there are complications during the third trimester, attempt to remain calm. Talk about what you are feeling, and try to be positive. Pray together, and reaffirm your appreciation and respect for your wife. I can tell you first-hand that receiving disappointing news from doctors and nurses about the pregnancy is strenuous. Your mind races, and you immediately go to the worst-case scenarios. We have received news of placenta previa, malpositioned babies, concerning blood levels, worrisome vital signs, mysterious cells on biopsies, and everything in between. Just know that many times, doctors and nurses are wrong. They are doing the best they can with the diagnostics and experience that they have, but they are still fallible humans. When there is a legitimate problem, there is likely a remedy.

My wife's grandmother, Nita, was told that she would certainly die if she tried to give birth to her daughter (my mother-in-law). This dreadful diagnosis came after a previous son was born with major complications that resulted in childhood death. In an act of faith, courage, and true devotion, Nita let the doctor know that she would not terminate a pregnancy. She said that if she, herself, died in the process, that she would accept that. My mother-in-law was born without any problems to either party, and as a result, I received an incredible wife years later. Either the doctors miscalculated, or there was a miracle. Both can certainly occur, and they happen every day.

We have anguished over the news and potential problems many times, but we have been delighted to find that many of them never manifested in any tangible issue. We had a breech baby flip at the last second, long after doctors said it wasn't possible. We have had bad biopsies of lesions that just later disappeared. We witnessed the delivery of a badly damaged placenta, preceded by a perfectly normal baby delivery and totally healthy child. We continue to see a child that was diagnosed with severe, possibly fatal, brain damage, perform normally his entire life without any problems. Miracles? Misdiagnoses? You decide. I like believing the prior. Nonetheless, keep fighting, and keep praying.

8 HOURS BC

It's Go Time

It's time. It's finally time! 15 minutes, 9 minutes, 6. Pain.

Yes! Let's do this. Oh man, here we go! Are we ready?

We? Am I ready?

Too late, time to go! Pretend that you know what to do.

So you are waiting and waiting and then finally, contractions start getting more frequent and more intense. I know we covered some of this before, but I want to reiterate that most every woman thinks she is in labor before she actually is, especially the first time around. That fact will make no difference to you or your wife when action starts. It's an intense situation, and it should still be taken seriously. If it's the real thing, don't worry, we have a plan. To confirm that it's not a false alarm, you need to keep an accurate log of what's happening. Write down the time when a contraction starts, how long it lasts, and then record a pain rating on a scale from 1 to 10, with 10 being the worst. There's got to be an app for that. The pain scale will change in the very near future, but for now, just write what she says. Call the hospital or OB on call when she thinks she's starting labor. By then, you should have a pretty good record in the log of what has been happening with her contractions. They will ask you how many, how often, and how intense the contractions have been over the last hour. They are looking for frequent, consistent, intensifying events that indicate real labor. Increasing pain is a significant sign. In a real labor contraction, a woman probably cannot speak in the middle of it because of the pain. Initially, the hospital staff may tell you not to come yet, but to wait until the events are closer together or more intense, or whatever their criteria is. For liability sake, some facilities make you come in every time you call. Just be cool, keep an accurate record, and follow the instructions from the professionals. When you reach the limits that they told you to look out for, it's time to move. The criteria for heading to the hospital usually includes a painful, consistent contraction, that is repeating every five minutes or less. The timing depends on how far along you are in the pregnancy, how far you are from the hospital, and a few other possible factors unique to this pregnancy. The doctor or midwife will let you know the criteria. When it's time, execute the plan. Don't freak out and forget something in a panic, but don't dilly-dally either.

If you are prepared, just grab the pre-packed bags and escort your hero wife to the vehicle of choice. Grab a cup of ice on the way out too. She may want it before you make it to the hospital. It's impossible to refrain from getting too excited during this part. Don't drive like a maniac or say anything stupid. Try to stay level-headed. Tend to every request from your woman, who is now in a state of shock and intense pain. Everything runs smoother if you are on your game. She needs to see you in control and confident in your preparation. Do not snap at her if she gets testy. Err on the side of being gracious and compassionate. She is in a bad state, and it's now escalating by the minute. Call the OB's office if you haven't done so already. Let them know your progress and request that they call the hospital to let them know that you are in labor and on the way. Next, call the hospital and let them know that you are on the way, that you just spoke with your doctor, and that you have already pre-registered. (You did that, right?) Stay calm, and be polite. Your attitude will certainly affect the way people will treat you. That goes for everything in life, especially events where you need nurses. The hospital workers have some major leverage over you. Do not give them any reason to dislike you. They are the gatekeepers to the room, the meds, and the professionals that you are so desperately seeking. Be kind, speak softly, and be grateful. "Yes, ma'am" and "thank you" go a long way. Your model behavior will be remarkable in contrast to the other couples that are barking orders and impulsively expressing the first thing that comes to mind. Don't be surprised if you get to quietly skip a few of those people in line. Acting like a frustrated drill sergeant never helps.

When you arrive at the hospital, you will likely be disappointed that no one else but you two think this is an urgent matter. Remember, they see excited couples every day, and most of the time, they send the expectant parents back home because of a false alarm. Either way, stick to the plan, and make your way to the check-in desk. Let them know again that you have already pre-registered and that your wife is most definitely in active labor. It is also good to mention that you just got off the phone with (namedrop) your OB/GYN, and she should have already called to let the staff know that you were on the way to have this baby. They still will not be in a hurry unless your new child is literally hanging from your wife's nightgown. Don't worry. You likely have more time than you think, and if not, at least you are in the proper building to handle everything now.

There are some misconceptions about what to expect when her water breaks. This is when the amniotic sac ruptures, signaling that it's probably time to have a baby. Your girl has probably been having fears and bad dreams about this happening in the grocery store or in the communion line at High Mass. Contrary to what we hear and see in movies and not-so-much-reality shows, it is actually rare to happen in this fashion. If it does, it's not Niagara Falls as people will inaccurately portray it—it's usually just a trickle. Sometimes her water will break at home. Sometimes it happens en route to the hospital. Most times it happens naturally, in the hospital bed, after a series of heavy contractions. If it does not happen naturally, the doctor will manually break her water by inserting a piercing instrument when it's time for labor and delivery. It's not a big deal. They will let you know when it's time. This is actually encouraging because it means that things are about to speed up.

Back to the hospital check-in. Eventually, they will get you to a room and hook up all the usual monitoring equipment. You will probably be disappointed that this doesn't look like a room where you should have a baby. That's because it's not the final destination. This is the monitoring room where you will likely sit for 10-90 minutes, watching your wife get increasingly more uncomfortable, wondering if anyone is even watching the monitors at the nurse's station down the hall. You may be sharing this space with a few other couples. The staff is still just weeding out the patients that are not in real labor yet. Again, they will not have the same urgency as you two would prefer. The waiting really sucks for you. It's hard to watch your wife in pain and know that there is little that you can offer to help. The discomfort only increases with time, and so does your blood pressure. Don't get mad at the staff. Just be present to and compassionate for the mother of your child. Let her know that you are grateful for her and proud of her. Providing a hand to squeeze and a sip of cold water may be all you can offer. As things progress, and the painful situation starts escalating, you will get moved to a room where people actually birth babies. If your wife is planning to have an epidural, which you know I support 100%, it's OK to remind the nurse a time or two that you definitely want one as soon as possible. My wife would order her epidural before we even got in the car to go to the hospital if it were an option. She constantly, but tactfully, reminds each new person who enters the room that she is ready for it ASAP.

After rolling into the new spot, which likely has a little more space and a few cooler gadgets around, it is officially go time. It's likely that you still won't see your doctor or midwife for quite a while, but at least you are in a room that is labeled "Labor and Delivery." You are already laboring. Now it's time to achieve the second part—delivery. It's likely not quite time yet, and as you anxiously watch the hospital staff come and go, there is still no sign of someone who actually delivers humans from the birth canal. More monitoring, prepping, measuring, and waiting ensues. Remember, the goal is 100% effacement and 10 centimeters dilation. That's when the pushing starts. The wait for these two stats could be non-existent or last for more than a day. Be forewarned, it often takes longer with the first baby. Sometimes, the staff will get the laboring mother to sit up, change positions, take a walk down the hall, or do a CrossFit™ routine to move things along. Activity and pressure can help speed up the pace and convince the labor to kick into the next gear. They will let you know if it's a good idea to change anything. Don't do any box jumps or kettle bell swings with her without professional permission. The excursion from 4 centimeters to 10 is not fun to watch. Your wife will be hurting in a way that she cannot have prepared for. You feel useless standing there while she does all the work and endures all the pain. It sucks. But once the epidural is in, everything is cool again. It's magical and has to be on the top of the list of modern medicine's greatest breakthroughs. Sure, delivery can be done without it, and most certainly has been done that way many, many times. I personally don't want my wife to have to ever deliver without one.

In the event that an induction was scheduled and labor was accurately anticipated, the doctor may have prescribed an enema about 12 hours before delivery. This is a simple, over-the-counter, liquid laxative treatment. It's self-injected into the rectum (at home) and functions to totally empty the tank. Any stool that is in there will come out with astonishing efficacy. Every bowel movement makes more room for the baby. In theory, this should make delivery easier and cleaner. These methods also make it easier for the new mother to have a bowel movement after delivery, which sometimes can be a difficult feat.

4 HOURS BC

Things Just Got Real

Everything in my body was freaking out. I thought I was going to pass out or throw up, or do both. I was so excited and so nervous at the same time. Was I ready to be a dad? What if there are problems with the delivery? What if there is something wrong with the baby? Why isn't anyone else as concerned as I am? Deep breath... poker face... words of encouragement... focus... oh man... here we go!

The big show has arrived. It's not only D-Day, but it's also the final hour! The doctor may not be in sight yet, but the rest of the crew is prepping for the inevitable event that is about to commence. Every now and then someone checks the signs, the dilation, effacement, and contractions. The staff will let your wife know when a contraction is coming and how to deal with it. Stay by her side, and do whatever helps her. Don't lounge on the lousy sofa and check your phone notifications while she does all the work. Even if she doesn't want you to "help," be fully present. Use the phone to send updates when she asks you to. Otherwise, stay 100% focused on her. You already know this stuff by now, right?

Finally, she's 10 centimeters dilated and fully effaced. Her water has broken, and it's time to start pushing. This is usually when the delivery doc shows up. Her body position is quickly changed to accomodate delivery, and several people are now getting very up-close and personal with your wife. The staff watches for an incoming contraction on the digital monitor. Once it sets in, she is asked to push. Each push lasts about ten seconds, although sometimes the staff counts painfully slowly. After the ten-second push, she will be instructed to take a deep breath and then do it again. The pushing and breathing cycle will be repeated for as long as the contraction lasts. During each contraction, which is now happening every few minutes, she will push a few times. She will probably average three sets of pushes on each contraction. Then after the contraction passes, she rests for a brief moment and catches her breath. When the next one starts coming in, more pushing ensues. There will be some play-by-play updates and instructions by the staff, and hopefully a few words of encouragement all along the way.

If your wife has maintained top-notch health during the pregnancy, her diligence and discipline will pay big dividends in this phase. The pushing will be easier, which means a faster labor and less time for the baby to be in the canal. Because she chose to eat healthily and exercise, she is strong and has endurance. She and your baby will have a much easier time during the delivery and will have decreased the risk of complications.

Suddenly, your new baby starts coming into view. He emerges for the first time into the outside world in an adrenaline pumping, endorphin rich moment. Nothing in your life is comparable to this, and there is no way to predict how your body will respond to the moment. Just like the other hacks, prepare for the worst and hope for the best.

In your case, this means preparing for the possibility of you throwing up or passing out. Keep a chair close by and a trash can in reach. These things usually only happen to the people who think it would never happen to them.

Hopefully, the first thing that emerges is a head, face down, which is the easiest and most favorable position to deliver. Babies can arrive face up, feet first, transverse, or in many other positions. Special considerations must be made if the position is not ideal. Thanks to modern medical equipment, the position is hardly ever a surprise anymore. If a baby is in an unfavorable orientation, the doc will probably have known for weeks and planned accordingly.

The medical equipment will be measuring many things beyond just the contractions before and during active labor and the pushing phase. Blood pressure and heart rate, for both Mom and baby, will be monitored carefully. The staff will keep tabs on these items and respond accordingly. You will certainly hear beeps and notification alarms. Don't panic. If either of these gets out of ideal range, some changes will be made to reduce the risk of injury.

Often, the baby is too large, or the opening is too small, to deliver smoothly. These difficulties are more common with baby number one and with later term deliveries. One way the doctor can increase the size of the opening is by performing an episiotomy on Mom, which means cutting a slit in the soft tissue on the bottom side of the business district. It's common and not too invasive. It's done with a scalpel or sterile scissors and only takes a few seconds. Sometimes the deliverer needs less than an inch, and sometimes she needs several.

Either way, the goal is to increase the size of the opening to deliver the baby through in a timely fashion. Afterward, this area will be sutured back together. It will add a little extra healing time, but it is a common procedure that shouldn't make you too nervous.

Sometimes, the baby doesn't move adequately, and there needs to be some pulling assistance from outside to accompany the pushing from inside. Pulling may be assisted by a suction device or forceps. A vacuum-like device provides suction with a cup-shaped tip that attaches to the baby's head, allowing the doctor a way to gently pull the baby through and manipulate the position as the child moves. Forceps are like a specialized set of salad tongs. They are curved to fit around the baby's head, again allowing for the doctor to gently pull while Mom pushes.

If these and other methods are not enough, the last resort is a C-Section. As you already know, a cesarean section is an operating room procedure where the abdomen and uterus are surgically opened so the baby can be safely delivered without needing to pass through the birth canal. Sometimes, based on health concerns, baby size, or compromised position, the doctor knows that a C-section is necessary before labor even starts. Other times, it can be a spur of the moment decision based on how the delivery is playing out. A C-section is not the end of the world. It will certainly add procedures to the final hospital bill and add more recovery time afterward, but it's sometimes the safest option for the baby. If this is necessary, don't panic. With modern day medicine, the baby is much safer outside with proper medical attention than inside the womb.

Oh, and one more thing. All of that pushing can cause many substances to be forced out of your beloved bride during labor. If she hasn't been a little embarrassed by now, there is a massive potential that she will be, yet again. I don't want to be crude or graphic, but just know that there may be some urinary or fecal discharge at some point. It may surprise both of you, but not the staff. You should be mentally ready for that so that you can act like a professional, and not look shocked or grossed out. No smiling or joking either. Suppress your middle school self if he still exists. There are much greater things to get excited about at a time like this, right?

0 BC / 0 AD

D-Day: Party of Three

I suddenly started feeling an intense heat followed by an immediate cold sweat. The nurse looked over and said, "Are you OK?" I confidently said that I was fine. She kept counting, with one eye on me and one on her work. She was holding a leg in position, still cheering my wife on and counting to ten. After the contraction, she leaned over and whispered in an unmistakable tone, "Sit your butt down, Daddy!"

Whether by pushing, pulling, or surgical retrieval, at some point, a baby is coming into view. As we said before, we hope that the first sight is the top of a tiny head, face down, moving through the birth canal. You must try to prepare yourself for the sights of the delivery room. If it isn't enough to see the pain, pushing, pulling, stretching, spreading, and everything else, the sight of your baby is very overwhelming. You've been waiting a long time for this special gift. Only this gift, unlike the ones you opened on a spry Christmas morning long ago, also scares the heck out of you. It ignites more powerful hormones and carries much more weight. Viewing the sonogram photo is an amazing moment but pales in comparison to the real thing. The reality of being a dad hits you crazy hard the first time you see the little guy in the flesh. You may find yourself speechless, very emotional, or sick. The staff will be coaching you and your wife and probably reminding you to breathe too. Your job is strictly to support your wife. Try to enjoy it for what it is. After all, this is the biggest moment in your life.

First, the top of a little head, then his full head, then the shoulders, the torso, the pelvis, and finally, some seemingly undersized legs and feet. Whew! That was a lot. It may take three seconds or many, very long minutes. Someone is now holding your child. He is here. If you feel the least bit queasy at any point in this circus, sit down. Have a cold soda or some juice close by in case of a drop in blood sugar and the feeling of overheating. This is the only time I support having a sugary soda. If you make it through standing, now is the time to kiss your wife. Thank her. Tell her you love her. She will never forget this moment. Be brief, kind, and supportive. Allow her to take in all the profound, life-changing moments. Compliment the beautiful child and the beautiful woman who just promoted you to your new position.

The staff will use a bulb suction to remove amniotic fluid, blood, and other goop from the little guy's nose and mouth. This is standard procedure and sometimes can look a little aggressive. They will then likely ask you if you want to cut the cord. That's what dads do in the L&D suite, so they have one thing to brag about later when lighting the cigars. It's a nice way that the staff includes you and gives you some attention. You can deny this process if you choose, and the pros will handle it. Just know that if it were a procedure that you could screw up, they would not offer it to you. They usually put two clamps on the cord, and you snip in between the pre-set landmarks. Either you or someone else cuts the cord and makes sure one clip stays with the baby. The physical connection is officially severed, just as the emotional and spiritual connection spike to record levels. A very quick wipe down commences, and the new baby is placed in the overwhelmed and overjoyed mother's arms. It's incredible. If you didn't believe in God before, you likely do now, and you should. This work of art is miraculous. So many seemingly impossible things have to come together for this to all work. Your identities and your roles changed nine months ago, but suddenly it's so much more intense and remarkable. Your hero bride has been anticipating this moment for a long time, and it's way better than she ever imagined. The first major leg of the journey is now complete. Congrats, man!

1 HOUR AD (AFTER DELIVERY)

The After Party

After the party, it's the after party.

Your baby is finally here. The celebration can begin, but there is still some unfinished business that needs to take place before we can call it a wrap and head for the door. One order of business that guys may not be ready for, and possibly never knew about, is delivering the afterbirth. Afterbirth consists mostly of the placenta and cord, plus some fluids. You need to know about this so that you don't think you are having unexpected twins. The shocking part for many guys is not just that this process happens, but how remarkable the placenta is. Most first-time dads have never seen anything like it, in books or real life. It's big. Like, almost as big as the baby, big. It's bright purple and dark red, with blood vessels stretching over the exterior surface. It's like something out of a sci-fi alien movie. Prepare yourself by viewing a few pictures online beforehand and reading up on it. Delivering the non-baby products can take just a minute or two, or be a thirty-minute process.

The final task is cleaning and dressing the site. Finishing the delivery process may require that the doctor puts in a few stitches or applies medications to facilitate better healing. Sutures are usually necessary if an episiotomy was performed, and sometimes are needed for unintended wounds that resulted from the delivery.

There's nothing to get too worked up about on either of these housekeeping issues. I just want you to know what's going on so you can be attentive to all of it. I know it's a lot. You'll do fine. Most of this part will be going on while you watch the new arrival get measured, checked, warmed, and washed on the other side of the room.

Most women donate the placenta to be used for research and other medical purposes. You will likely have been asked to sign a paper concerning this well before it was lying in a stainless steel pan. You don't have to sign anything over if you don't want to. Some women prefer to keep it and do all types of things with it, like bury it in the garden. Some groups advocate eating it. Yes, I said eating it. I don't know how, why, or when, but apparently, some people do it. Every time I enter a discussion on this topic with someone other than my wife, I get myself in trouble. Personally, we have always elected to donate the placenta for research and not bring it home. I have no further comment on this subject.

You may have never seen the phenomenon before, but you must know about the cone heads. I'm not talking about the Dan Aykroyd skit on SNL, but now that we mentioned it, keep that image in your mind. If labor and delivery last a long time, and the baby is in the birth canal for an extended period, the little guy is likely to have a cone head when he finally emerges. If the baby is delivered with an elongated cranium, don't freak out. He is not going to look like your father-in-law for long. It is temporary. It's just an incredible, superior design for survival. Unlike an adult skull that is hard all the way around, a newborn's head is much softer and has movable parts. The human skull is made up of several hard plates, but babies have not developed the bony connection between these plates yet, which means their heads can change shape as pressure is applied. This is an incredible feat that allows the skull to become thinner and longer so it can move through the canal more easily. In the days and weeks following the delivery, the plates will move back into place, resulting in a more rounded and less torpedo-like shape.

Hustle and Bustle

Whew! It's done. A new member has officially been inducted into the family. Now what the heck are we supposed to do?

The new baby is here, and many tasks have been initiated. Length, weight, temperature, and blood pressure measurements must be recorded and monitored. Eye drops, heat lamps, swaddle wraps, pricks, sticks, medicines, blue lights, lotions, and soaps are all being used in a controlled but rapid fashion. You should be present to witness all of it, which probably means that you will be across the room from your heroine wife that is finishing up with her remaining housekeeping procedures. Talk to your little guy. Touch him and allow him to hear your voice. You are the father of a new, amazing person. Try to take it all in, even though it may feel surreal and bizarre to you. The reality of all of it hasn't quite set in yet. If you have questions for the medical staff, now is the time to ask. Feel free to do so. Ask what you can do to help out. Be present. Take pictures, but don't experience this incredible day exclusively behind your phone or camera. Soak it all in, in real time. This is reality, not a reality show. Don't forget to check on Mom too. She will be busy for a few minutes, but will certainly want to see what's going on and get a play-by-play update from you. Some of the first steps are tough to watch, especially shots and pricks. He's just so tiny, innocent, and so vulnerable.

The red heat lamp that looks like it should have french fries under it is there to help regulate body temperature. It seems a little hot, but remember, the little guy just left a very warm, 98.6-degree environment. He is now in a much cooler room and doesn't yet have much body fat for insulation. The other light that may be used in the same room is blue and helps to prevent and treat jaundice.

If you elected to slow down, postpone, or eliminate any vaccine schedules, you might want to remind the nurses of that now. Don't be a pushy know-it-all or give them any lectures about your personal views of vaccines or politics. Be polite, and just make sure that they know your wishes. Otherwise, they may run through the habitual, standard routine that they have done 10,000 times before. Do some research and due diligence on the types of recommended immunizations, the scheduling options, and the risks and benefits for each one. Vaccinations are a highly debated topic right now, and they deserve adequate discernment. It's the parents' choice to decide what to receive, what to deny, and what to postpone. Personally, after much education and discernment on the subject, we choose to space out vaccinations and receive them more slowly that the typical schedule for our children. To make your decision on the matter, read credible research and talk to professionals and, ultimately, do what feels best for you and your new family.

The nurses will complete some official paperwork and likely some sentimental, souvenir items as well. If you have a baby book (you probably don't, but your wife does), get them to stamp the footprints in it when they are doing that step of the paperwork. Amazingly, they still use actual ink and real paper for this. Take pictures or videos of everything, especially those significant one-time things like the first time Mom holds the baby, footprints, first bath, etc. Once again, I will remind you not to stop to share these items yet! Saturate yourself in the moment. We've been over this, right? The world can wait, and the people in it do not care as much about this as either one of you anyway. If possible, designate a loved one to do the picture-taking and video-making so that you are fully experiencing each step of the life-altering process. These digital timepieces will be a wonderful source of reflection later. They may even be an effective tool for bonding when you need to be reminded of your family love and marriage commitments. You will need some extra reminders from time to time over the next few decades. Trust me.

Once all the medicines, vital signs, and checkups are complete, everything starts to slow down. Emotions start to regulate, and the reality of being a parent starts to emerge. Now, it's time for a good bath. Everybody in the room probably needs one, but I am specifically talking about the baby's first bath. A seemingly aggressive scrub will commence, resulting in a clean little human that resembles your family members, but probably smells much better. In time, you will learn how to bathe, diaper, and swaddle the baby just like the pros are doing in front of you. Don't worry too much about it right now. You will have a few days' worth of help before you have to go solo. Just enjoy it for what it is. Once all the chores are done, your new baby will be swaddled tightly and handed back to you. Your baby is likely starting to calm down now because he is back in a warm, tight position, much like the environment he's grown accustomed to over the last few months in the womb. If Mom is finished with her duties and is ready, walk the little nugget over and give him to her. If she isn't ready quite yet, just enjoy holding him. You can gently sway and shush while he is in your arms in the swaddle. Being back in a warm, snug position is pure gold to a new baby.

Once your all-star wife and prized newborn are both well and all cleaned up, you will hopefully be ready to move to your third and final room. It's officially recovery time, and all three of you will need some.

Catch Your Breath

We rolled her into an 87-degree room with chipping paint and a flickering overhead light. I saw the broken "dad chair" in the corner with the footrest dangling, and I knew I was screwed for the next 48 hours.

As long as everything is in check, the only thing left to do is rest and recover. What an understatement, right? At least you aren't missing half of the internal contents that your body was housing 120 minutes ago. There will likely be a mixed feeling of relief and fear going into the recovery room. You are relieved that everything went well, but scared that something could still go wrong. This person seems so fragile and needy. Not to mention your wife and the baby.

Depending on the hospital, the recovery room may be less than desired. I have been in hospitals that were similar to the Four Seasons and ones that more closely resembled a county jail cell. Two people will be guaranteed a warm, moderately soft bed. Neither of those two people will be you. There will likely be a bad recliner or maybe an undersized sofa for you. I think they call those things a love seat, but you won't be feeling the love. Regardless of your back pain and potential lack of slumber, do not complain. I repeat, do not complain. It sucks to be uncomfortable, but remember, you didn't just have a nine-pound person removed from your body. I do recommend asking the nurse (or several of them as they change shifts) if there is a better chair somewhere that you could move into the room. Ask politely letting the nurse know that you want to be present in the room, at your wife's side, for everything. You know, like a real, compassionate husband and awesome new dad would do. You are an anomaly to what they see every day, and they will likely want to be kind to you for being so. A lot of guys go home or get a hotel, but you will be there, right beside your wife. Stay there, sleep there, help out, and go the distance. Don't outsource this duty to a family member unless the adult patient in the room explicitly tells you to do so. Better yet, don't do it unless she tells you the second time. She probably didn't mean it the first time anyway. You need to be there for her and your new baby. I know that you would not have even considered sleeping in a more luxurious place, but I had to remind you just in case you were tempted. You have a few important things to learn, but truthfully, your biggest job is to be present and attentive.

In recovery, you will mostly be hanging out while Mom and baby both sleep. New babies sleep a whole lot, and your wife's body is beyond exhausted. Your child will be rolled in and out from time to time for tests, checkups, and rest. The best rest for Mama will come when the baby is in the nursery, but the times when he is in your room will be very special. I want to say something that may surprise you, which is, for the first two nights, send the baby to the nursery for 6-8 hours if they will let you. You will have plenty of all-nighters when you get home, so use your evenings at the hospital to sleep. I promise he won't feel neglected and remind you of it when he's 17 years old. Use the help now while you have it. You are paying for it. Your wife needs good rest for a better and faster recovery. You will still be awakened multiple times each night for meds, blood pressure checks, and shift changes. The sound of Velcro™ ripping on a blood pressure cuff is always offensive at 2:00 a.m., but it will be done with the same intense vigor every few hours whether you are ready for it or just hitting your first REM sleep in a week. During the day, keep the baby close by as much as possible. Use that time to learn how to change, feed, burp, and swaddle from the staff. Hold him, speak to him, and just let him be in the room sleeping with the both of you. He will learn to sleep with noise and be comforted by your voices.

1 DAY AD

The Calm Before the Storm

This place is nothing like the all-inclusive resort you saved up all those vacation days to visit.

You've been through a lot, and you may have forgotten about your other job. Now is the time to call in and arrange some time off work. Hopefully, there are some vacation days, sick days, or paternity leave time that you can use. Regardless of whether you prepared in advance for this, it's time to be with your family. Some guys don't take off work at all, and many others take an insufficient amount of time and can't wait to get back. You, in contrast to the status quo, are an exceptional guy that will be more available and more hands-on than the male populous. Take some time off. Be present. Do the hard work.

If you have a considerable amount of leave time to use, I recommend using it in multiple waves, instead of one long stint. You certainly need to be around for the next few days, if not the whole week. However, if one of the baby's new grandparents or relatives plans to visit and help in the next few weeks, maybe you should let Grandma fill in for a few days so that you can be home later when the other help has expired. Your wife may appreciate it more too. Instead of having a house full of eager people, maximize your time to overlap the void. If it's possible, take a few of your days in week two and a few in week three or four to create extra-long weekends. You can decide what works best for your specific situation. Just know that sometimes you are needed more after the donated meals and friendly help dissipates. If there is no way to take off work, ask your employer and staff if you can complete some of your work from home.

Another item that you need to go ahead and take care of is letting your insurance company know that you have a new family member that needs to be added to your policy. The little guy won't have a social security number yet, but he needs to be added to the plan as soon as possible. From this point on, he is a patient that will be billed for his own list of services. Just give them a call and give the information they need. Adding a new dependent is standard procedure and only takes a few minutes.

Complications Are Complicated

After two miscarriages and nine agonizing months of a high-risk pregnancy that had been ravaged by fear and anxiety, he was finally here, and he was dying. Everything in my being was imploding, and people needed me more than ever. For the first time in my life, I had no energy. It would have been infinitely easier for me just to disappear, but that wasn't an option.

Complications of any kind can emerge before, during, or after childbirth. Issues can range from very mild and temporary to life altering and devastating. My family has been exposed to some heartbreaking and terrifying events over the years. There is no fear and panic like the news of a baby or a mother in trouble. Whether it's a little extra bleeding, an infection, breathing issues, deformations, unfavorable tests, broken body parts, or worse, expect it to be the most difficult undertaking you have ever faced. It will be extremely trying for you and your wife. If an unfavorable event comes your way, give it the adequate respect and attention that it deserves.

The key to surviving these moments is having information, support, and faith. If you are missing any or all of them, it can feel impossible to overcome. Even if you have all three elements in place, it can be a treacherous ordeal. It may still feel like you are suffocating. Being informed gives you some sense of control, even though you have very little. If you have an amazing doctor, nurse, or midwife, they will sympathize with you and attempt to keep you calm and in the loop.

Ask questions, and keep asking until you understand the situation. Be careful what you read online as many sites that will come up in your searches will be inaccurate. You need valid, valuable insight pertaining to these complications, and it needs to be gathered from credible, professional sources. Knowledge is power. If you don't know about jaundice, and you heard it diagnosed for the first time concerning your six pounds of unbelievable love, it sounds horrible. When you find out that it happens all day, every day, and the treatment is a warm spot under a special lightbulb, suddenly you can breathe again. If it's something bigger and more debilitating, you will still need information to lessen the state of panic and anxiety.

Family support is invaluable, not only because of the immediate need to be surrounded by more love, but because the other people around you are probably thinking more clearly at the moment and can provide some sound encouragement and support. They can also bring you a good meal, do some research, have conversations with hospital staff, or just be there, so that you aren't alone. Don't deny the people that you love the opportunity to be there, unless they are complicating the situation. Some family members have a keen ability to do this.

In times like these, faith may be your only saving grace. Regardless of how strong your faith has been in the past, you will quickly need to step it up and use it in many new capacities. You will voraciously search within yourself to find strength to cope. That faith may be used for gratitude, hope, joy, graceful suffering, desperate pleas for help, or some other deep need. If your faith has been on the sidelines for a while, it's about to be called in to perform in the big leagues. Your family will need you to be a spiritual leader forever. This won't be the last time you need strong faith. My only advice is to communicate with God, and because communication is always a two-way street, speak your heart and also take time to listen to God's response. Use your faith to full capacity so that you can be the rock that your family needs in a tough time. Someone needs to remain unshaken and grounded. The family will instinctively turn to you as a leading father and husband. Although suffering is a part of life, and we will all suffer at some point, we can take pride in suffering gracefully with a heart full of love and devotion. I have been in some seemingly dark and hopeless times when it seemed I had nothing but despair. I felt useless, which made me more depressed, unfulfilled, and vulnerable. What I have learned is that at some point, we have to decide to be on the offense. Instead of just receiving blow after blow until we can no longer stand, we should be proactive, positive, and prayerful. Then, regardless of the outcome, you can be proud and non-remorseful about the way you handled it.

With each new development, ask yourself, "What is the most loving response that I can have at this moment?" Try your best to react in a thoughtful way, giving yourself to the people that need you. Now we are talking about being a real man and being the leader that your family needs. You weren't trained for this, but you can and must take the job and face it head on. It would be easier to die, but that isn't an option. You've always known that you were designed for something great. You can't stop now.

The Last Place You Expected to Be

You come in to visit, desperately hoping for good news. You do whatever you can to cope and pretend to be stronger than you are for your wife. Then you are asked to leave, to leave your newborn baby suffering and struggling. You must exit as the shift changes, and a new wave of caregivers comes in. You size them up in a quick glance to try to evaluate their character, see who is compassionate and capable enough to minister to your child's needs. You can't do anything but stand there and watch people do their work. It's routine for them, and gut wrenching for you. If you don't regularly talk to God, you are about to start, and it may not be in the kindest tone.

My sincere hope is that this chapter will never be relevant to you. If you never have to visit a sick child, I will celebrate with you. However, it's still necessary for me to write it, and for you to read. You may find my advice useful now for an immediate situation with your baby. It could apply later in situations with other parents that you know and love who are stuck in a difficult situation. This section involves complications with the baby that warrant special medical attention in the Neonatal Intensive Care Unit (NICU). I have personally been there, and I can attest that it absolutely stinks to have to spend time in the unit.

A visit to the NICU can range from minor and routine to severe or fatal. There are babies in the unit that just need extra blue light and a day of monitoring, and some that are hanging on to life by a tiny thread for months. It's tough to be in there and see babies, often only a pound or two, that are struggling to survive. It's heartbreaking to see the other parents. But it's horrible when you are the parents, and the baby in front of you on the life-preserving equipment is your own. Nothing prepares you for this because your expectation was a warm, sleeping, tightly swaddled little person in your arms. Not being able to hold your child is awful, and seeing him with multiple tubes and wires running in and out of his little body is even worse. These times are unimaginably difficult to handle.

I'm going to give some practical advice and some encouragement. I have been through some seemingly impossible odds and horrible diagnoses with my wife, with one of my sons, and with several newborns in my extended family. These tasks are simple in theory, but invaluable to the battle at hand.

1. Stay positive.

This is easy to say, but hard to practice. Speak with hopeful words and tone. Know that these NICU's are amazing. With the help of modern medicine, advanced techniques, and state-of-the-art equipment, they can do seemingly impossible things to save a baby's life and bring him back to good health. Despite overwhelming odds, I have seen many children come through early difficulties and end up just fine. One of my sons experienced full healing with no long-term problems, even after horrific brain scan results and an inability to breathe on his own for days. Regardless of the diagnosis, know that there is hope for a full recovery.

2. Be present.

It will feel like there is not much that you can do to help, and that fact drives most guys crazy. This helpless feeling is difficult to manage, especially for new dads. If you are like most men, you want to take charge and fix things. In this case, though, you have to just wait and rely on others. That waiting is tough. However, be as present as possible to this situation and especially to your wife. Visit your little guy as much as the NICU will allow. Allow family members to be there if you need to be away for some time. Call for updates during the non-visiting hours. Let your family and the staff see you doing the work. It will motivate everyone to be stronger. It will also give you a much-needed sense of purpose.

3. Pray.

This may naturally happen out of necessity or desperation, but I want to encourage you to take it a step further. There are many benefits to prayer and meditation. Praying aloud with your spouse and over your child is very powerful too. I have witnessed several indisputable miracles in my life during prayer. I have been the direct recipient of some unbelievable and miraculous things. But even in the absence of definitive proof of divine happenings, developing a habit of praying is beneficial. We need to be grateful, to reflect, to be honest, and to get a few things off of our chests. We need to get in touch with our new vocation and learn how to listen. In the times that you feel like you can't do anything to help a difficult situation, pray. Sometimes I don't feel like doing it either, but it's always beneficial when it's done. Praying allows you to at least do something other than just sit there.

That something is needed, for all parties involved. It doesn't have to be profound or poetic, just honest. You can't do it wrong.

4. Ask for Support.

Rally whatever troops that you have in your network for support. Reach out to friends, family, and relatives, and let them know what is going on. It makes a huge difference when other people come together in support of you and your family. Little gestures of love and kindness all have an impact on how you get through this phase. It may just be a few minutes to visit, a good meal delivered, an errand to run, or honest prayers that totally change your day. Allow people to do some of these things. Accept generosity if it is offered. Community can be a beautiful thing if your pride will allow it to work. You will need the help and will learn to appreciate it.

5. Rest.

During the times when visiting is not allowed, try to rest. It's hard when your brain is racing through scenarios and fears, but you and your spouse need rest. No one functions well when they are sleep-deprived. This stuff is mentally and physically exhausting, even if you are at your best, which you certainly won't be. Everything suffers when we are tired. Take visitation shifts with family if possible. You may need to take a sleep aid during the available rest periods to be able to truly relax and recover. Talk to your doctor, or try an over-the-counter aid to help get some rest. Benadryl™ or melatonin may be a good option for you. Your doctor may recommend a stronger sleep aid or even an anti-depressant or anti-anxiety drug. If you need some help, don't be ashamed or hesitant to seek it. My only recommendation is to stay away from any habit-forming or addictive drugs. Try to avoid depressants like alcohol. Discuss it with your doctor before you are at the end of your rope and totally burned out.

My advice may be easier said than done. There is no way to sugarcoat it. This topic is rough. Having your baby in the NICU is awful. When it's all over, and those professionals saved your newborn's life, you will be eternally grateful to them. They are a special breed of people. Not many people can do the work they do. Be sure to show appreciation for it. Bring goodies for them, or ask if they need coffee when you head out to get one. Let them see your diligence and gratitude. Hang in there. Try to be a solid rock until the storm passes, even if you don't feel strong enough.

Sticky Milestones

Um, do you have another pack of wipes for this diaper change? There are only 23 left in this one, and I think I need a few more.

Now that we covered the hard stuff that I pray you will never need, let's return to the expected routines for every baby. The first poop after delivery is a victory for the baby. It may be a big relief when mom has her first one too. It's common for women to have some painful trouble for a few days. The newborn's first bowel movement is one of the milestones that will be monitored by the staff. When this comes, it will probably be different from what you had expected, even if you have changed diapers before. The foreign stuff in the first movement is called meconium. It's different than all of the ones that will follow. It's so strange because it is made up of the substances that were ingested while in the uterus, which will never be consumed again. The first stool looks more like a tar ball from an oil spill than something that a human would produce. If an adult had a stool like this, they would speed to the nearest GI specialist to find out what went so horribly wrong inside of their digestive tract to produce such an alien substance. It's dark and sticky. No single baby wipe, or beach towel for that matter, will be sufficient to finish the changing job on this one. Each subsequent diaper will change as time goes on and things will normalize once the little guy is on a new meal plan. Just don't be alarmed with the toxic sludge-looking excrement when it arrives. You will handle it fine. I just wanted you to know about it. The hack that I have for this event is to use the interior of the diaper itself to wipe as much as possible, then move to as many baby wipes as you need. You may want to make a two-ply sheet by putting two wipes together. Over the first week, the matter will gradually transition from a dark, thick, black color to a thinner, yellowish substance. In time, the diaper changes will require fewer wipes and less facial grimacing from parents.

You Love 'Em. She Hates 'Em

The lactation consultant is a woman... right?

Feeding is a simple subject that can get dicey and blindside you before you ever knew what hit you. Hopefully, you have already discussed whether you plan to breastfeed, bottle feed, or a mixture of both.

Breastfeeding has been proven to be healthier for many reasons, and I encourage you to do your research. From nutrients, to immune defense, to hormonal benefits, breast milk is a superior product when it's available. Unless there is some serious physical or medical reason not to do so, everyone should probably give breastfeeding an honest try for their newborn. Many professionals, celebrities, and lay people have made it their mission to educate the world on the benefits, and there is some significant social and political clout that comes with the subject. It's like a religion to some people, and there is no shortage of dedicated evangelists. There can be a lot of pressure surrounding this process and choice too.

The truth is that many women have a terribly difficult time breastfeeding. The problem is that women don't know how hard it can be until they try it. Some ladies cannot breastfeed or are very limited because of prior surgery or trauma, hormonal troubles, nutrition problems, or anatomical issues. Babies can struggle with breastfeeding too. Some children can't get the technique down because of anatomy, muscle tone, pain, or other unforeseen complications. When it's difficult or impossible, a woman can get very upset and feel defeated or inferior. It can leave her feeling like she has failed as a new mother. When you turn on the atomic blender of emotions, hormones, and exhaustion, her feelings reach a nuclear level. This is the first major duty she has taken on as a mother, and if she feels as if it's not going to work, she will be upset. These feelings of inadequacy or defeat are common and can be seriously depressing for a mother. Don't be surprised at intense responses to the breastfeeding struggle.

Breastfeeding can also be physically painful. A mother may be able to work through the discomfort, and it become more bearable over time. Sometimes it's just a matter of building a tolerance for it or finding the right position. There are also some products on the market that can help ease the pain. Other times, it never improves, or it gets worse. Some women trudge ahead and endure the pain, and some simply cannot continue.

If your wife, who is recovering from a heroic and bloody war, gets harassed or disrespected by staff at the hospital, defend her. Do not let anyone bully her, belittle her, or discourage her. I'm speaking from direct experience after an impatient, aggressive nurse trampled over my wife in a time of difficulty. Some people champion breastfeeding to such an extent that they will act like fools, lacking compassion and empathy for a new mom who is trying her best to work it out. Encourage, cheer, support, and if needed, defend and fight for your wife. Let her know that you are proud of her, no matter what the outcome. Only one person can do this work. Give her the space to learn the skill, and acknowledge the sacrifice and struggle she is undertaking.

Regardless of your zeal for breasts and an eager willingness to help, your wife will probably still need some professional guidance. A breastfeeding coach of some sort will be available to assist in learning the proper techniques. Most hospitals call this a lactation consultant. I have no idea of the requirements to don this title, but I do not think that a medical degree is necessary. Nonetheless, a good breastfeeding trainer is one that is patient and encouraging. Hopefully it's a woman who has been through it a few times herself and maybe even had a hard time mastering it. A bad advisor can be downright mean and degrading. I recommend being there during all the training and trying. This will allow you to be both the bodyguard and the emotional support.

A valuable husband hack is to have a knowledge of what products are available to make breastfeeding easier. If you are a big time overachiever, anticipate there being some problems and have a bag of items already packed for the hospital beforehand. A trip or two to a supermarket or baby store will be very educational. There are products for pain, like covers, shields, and topical ointments. There are products for alignment and latching issues, like cups, shapers, and props. There are supplements for low flow, pads for leakage, and thermal pads for painful engorgement. None of these are very expensive, but one or two could make a big difference for that woman who is working so hard right now. If it all works easily for mom and baby right off, consider it a big blessing. Some women lack a sufficient supply of milk. Some newborns already have several teeth the day they are born. Ponder that for a minute.

The milk flow on the first few attempts will be sparse or even nonexistent. Healthy breast milk can take a few days to develop, and a delay should be expected. The milk production is based on hormone changes after delivery and takes time to work up to an adequate level. Pure breast milk usually takes a few days to show up, but breastfeeding is still necessary before it arrives. The first few precious drops to be consumed by the newborn are a thicker, yellowish substance called colostrum. It may have begun to ooze a bit before childbirth. This nutrient-rich, magical substance is premium fuel to a new baby. It's easy on his delicate digestive system and functions to eliminate bilirubin, which is the waste product of red blood cells that causes jaundice. It also helps produce the first meconium. Colostrum contains protective immune cells and antibodies that are passed from mother to baby and strengthens his immune system. This is like a built-in force field for infections and viruses. It's amazing stuff! So even if there is a bottle feeding plan for later, getting colostrum in your baby's system is a huge win and should be pursued. Every drop is beneficial.

You may be surprised to find out how little the baby actually eats during the first few days. He will typically lose a fair amount of weight in that time, which is normal, although you probably won't like the idea. You can discuss it with your pediatrician and your spouse, but I would recommend introducing some bottle feeding, even if the breastfeeding goes pretty well. My recommendation to do this serves three purposes: First, it takes some pressure off Mom to produce everything and to actually do all of the work alone. Second, it allows your newborn to learn how to drink from a bottle, which is a good skill to have when you need it. And third, it allows you to be a part of the process and to experience more quality time with the baby. This is an awesome bonding time for you, and it makes you more useful. When you are more useful, Mom gets more rest. Bottle feeding is a meaningful experience that you will probably learn to enjoy. You may even be sad one day when it's no longer needed. If all the feeding is the sole responsibility of the mother for the next few years, there will be some problems. Many women pull it off, but not without heartache, frustration, inconvenience, resentment, leverage, and exhaustion. Hopefully, she will appreciate your zeal and allow you to help. If so, all three of you win.

The staff will let you know when it's time to feed and will help out getting everyone on board, no matter what method you choose. Just so that you have a heads up now, the next few weeks will require feeding every few hours. Did you catch that? I mean like every two hours! That's all day and all night. Sometimes a feeding can take a full hour. So by now, an astute, masculine guy like yourself should realize that there will be no lengthy breaks for a while. It will gradually get longer and longer between feedings. You will make it to an easier routine eventually, but not immediately. Many dads are not expecting this demanding schedule. My goal is that you are fully prepared for it. You will be ready to handle it with a few hacks that I will share later.

In the coming days, the breast milk availability will increase. The baby's needs for the fluid will grow, and the supply volume will hopefully increase in proportion to the demand. Usually, as the milk supply increases, so do the size of her breasts. This may excite one, both, or neither of you. It may frighten one, both, or neither of you.

Just know that it's coming, and be respectful about it. Many women like the new changes to their breast size during pregnancy, then quickly despise the enlarged body parts when full milk production starts. If you are a typical male that produces testosterone, you will likely want to touch, and maybe grope, the newly up-sized objects. Be gentle. This can be a very painful time for her, especially in that area. The fuller they are, the more sore they become. Her nipples will likely be extremely tender, even at the lightest touch. Sometimes feeding is a great relief to her because of the decrease in pressure that can be so uncomfortable as it builds. Pumping may also be a great relief. We will cover that a little later, after you make it home.

Tiny Bottles and Big Burps

Eat, burp, spit up, burp, repeat. Not you, the baby!

The hospital staff will give you a hands-on demo to learn how to feed with a bottle. At first, only a tiny bit goes in between burping sessions. Drinking little sips and stopping for several minutes every half ounce to burp takes a while. This may be reminiscent of your old college days. Baby feeding is a time consuming endeavor. It can be testy and tedious. The repetitive routine can get tiring and boring. The baby's doctor will tell you the current time and volume goals for each feeding. Every baby is different, but your doctor will have a recommended target amount that your little guy needs to consume in order to thrive. This number will grow as the baby does. They will teach you the numerous ways to hold a baby while feeding, what warning signs to look for, and hopefully teach you several positions and techniques for burping your little one too.

I have no doubt that you will get the feeding part down. The hack that I want you to master is how to get good burps every time. There is a superior method. A lack of proper burping can cause discomfort for the child, more spit up, and hours of fussiness during and after feedings. Inadequate feedings and unrest from the baby leads to frustration, stress, and exhaustion for everyone. A tired, hungry, irritated human is hard to rationalize with, at any age. A good burping technique is paramount and will make feeding easier on everyone.

Over the years, I have mastered the burping methods and always get a happier, less messy, and more productive feeding session than when someone else does it. Either research online or ask someone on staff to teach you at least three positions for burping. The ace in the hole for me has always been to use a burping technique with the newborn in the sitting position. This is also the one that people use the least. Obviously, the baby can't sit up yet. He can't even hold his head up. What you do is sit him on your leg while you are in a comfortable seated position. He should be now "sitting" 90 degrees from your seated position, being supported by your thigh and hands. Let his legs sit toward the middle of yours. Make a C-shape with one hand, and cradle it under his chin, supporting his head, chest, and neck. Lean the little guy slightly forward with his face and torso resting on your hand. With the other open hand, you will gently pat him on the back. A lot of dads never learn this position. I have found that it will produce a burp when the traditional, over-the-shoulder position or the stomach position will not. For the best results, get proficient at each method, and use all three. If one spot isn't producing a good burp, change to another one for a bit. Alter the patting rhythm and position. Stop occasionally just to rub his back up and down with your open hand. If you notice that he's irritated and can't burp, pausing for a little bit just to get him horizontal usually helps. You will have to see what works best for him. It may be face up or face down (obviously without covering his face) that renders the best results. These little pauses help to change the air pressure in his little belly, and movement between the three positions helps get the air moving out. Mix it up until you master the process and learn the unique patterns for best results. Try not to force more fluids until you get a good burp. Putting extra volume on top of a big bubble will likely result in the baby returning it all on your lap when the burp finally rises to the top. One more hack related to feeding and burping is to keep a bag in the car with a change of clothes for all of you. You will need them at some point, or many points, over the next year when an unexpected bomb erupts from one end or the other.

Always have a burp cloth with you, especially if you are wearing your favorite polo or overpriced hipster shoes. These guys can expel a lot of fluid at any second. Always be ready for it. You will be impressed at the instantaneous trajectory and velocity that someone with such tiny muscles can produce. Keep the cloth in a smart catching position at all times, just make sure it's not blocking or covering his face. The one second that it's not in place will be the exact moment that you will get a crotch full of wet, vitamin-rich, milky goodness.

2 DAYS AD

Snip Snip

Delaying the circumcision for eight days suddenly seems like a genius proposition, and I'm not even Jewish.

If you do have a boy, you will have to make a decision on circumcision. Whether to do it, when to do it and whom should do it are all options that must be discussed. For families that just delivered a baby boy without religious reasons to defer the procedure, it's usually part of the standard process while at the hospital. Pay attention here. This hack is another money saver. It may also be a pain, blood, and bandage saver.

Most circumcisions are performed by the pediatrician that is making the daily rounds while your little one is in the nursery. If you want it done, your bundle of joy is on the daily list when the doc comes around. Your offspring, along with the other tiny newborn males on the list, all get the treatment during the rounds. You can ask specifics about the actual procedure, but I can tell you that they get it done quickly and efficiently. It is technically a surgery, but it's approached in a nonchalant sort of way—without sedation, anesthetics, or special operating rooms. It's a big deal for you to think about, but the staff will treat it as just another routine procedure. The thought of your perfect, extremely vulnerable, newborn son being cut with a scalpel is unnerving and a little heartbreaking. I don't have any big tips for how to deal with these sentiments. Sorry.

What I do have is a rarely considered hack that may make it considerably cheaper, and possibly reduce the healing time and potential complications. It's simple. Don't have it done at the hospital. Wait until a week later, and have it done at the next checkup with the pediatrician, in his or her office, or even with the OB/GYN. Yes, the OB. Here is my rationale:

When you have it done at the hospital, they will eagerly tack on a litany of hospital charges, including highly technical things like fees to "transport" the baby (pushing the cart) to the "surgical suite" (corner table of the nursery). They will also add aggrandized codes for the "sanitary surgical bed" (puppy pee pad), a "sterilization fee" (alcohol wipe), "infectious waste disposal" (tossing the aforementioned, soiled pad in the trash), "topical medicaments" (Vaseline™), "surgical dressing" (gauze and tape), "anti-inflammatory treatment" (cool water rinse), and who knows what else. All of these things look good on paper until you notice the premium pricing. My first two sons had $600–$1,200 worth of fees associated with their circumcision procedure alone. Both of them also had extended healing times and bleeding issues. I didn't know that at the time because I lacked a baseline comparison for the post-operative wounds and the recovery time. My latest two heirs to the family throne had this step done at the OB's office, a week later, after a well checkup, instead of at the hospital the day after being born. It was only about $300 there. Not only was it considerably cheaper, but it also looked beautiful and healed quickly.

Maybe it was a coincidence that the two procedures went so much smoother outside of the hospital. I think that it went better because of the setting and expectations. Instead of being one of nine procedures that needed to be done in an overbooked hour in the hospital nursery, Baby Dallas #4 was the only one they had to do that entire day, maybe even all week. The procedure wasn't rushed in the OB's office. I think that the operator wanted to do an exceptional job to impress us, and I think he was excited to use a skill set that demanded some expertise and attention to detail that he doesn't get to do every day. Ask your pediatrician and your OB what the options are for you.

Maybe it doesn't matter to you if you have full coverage insurance, but I would discuss it with both parties and go with the one that you are most confident in. After all, the sensitive body part they are operating on will be responsible for your family name one day.

While we are on the riveting topic of genitals, you may have noticed that he looks swollen or disproportionately large down there, which is probably nothing to worry (or brag) about. This condition is normal for newborns, both boys and girls, and will gradually change over the coming days.

Showing Up for the New Job

You've officially been promoted. You're ready to work and are certainly expected to. Now what? I thought you'd never ask.

It's a good thing that men are not solely responsible for the first 37 steps that occur in the first few hours of the little guy's life. There is no way we would pull it all off. Millions of people did it for centuries without the modern hospital staff, but my suspicion is that there were bunches of experienced and eager lady friends around who knew what to do while the men were panicking or missing. Be thankful for the conveniences and services that have been provided to your family. With that said, your list of responsibilities is now growing by the minute. It's your turn to start the official Dad duties. Besides the basics, like changing, feeding, and burping, you must have a few other skills that I believe are imperative to Dad success.

Now is the appropriate time to introduce the 5 "S's" that you need to know. I wish I could take credit for creating this hack, but it was crafted and refined many times over before I ever thought about it. The 5 "S's" are Swaddle, Swing/Sway, Shush, Side/Stomach, and Suck. These are found in the book, *The Happiest Baby on the Block*, by Dr. Harvey Karp. That book was by far the most useful one of many that I read on the subject of new babies. I do recommend it in the number two position, right behind *Hacking Fatherhood*, of course.

According to Dr. Karp, we can soothe an unsettled baby by trying to recreate the familiar environment of the womb. By doing this, it helps the baby feel more secure and calm. So we try to imitate the feel, sound, and habits that the baby has been peacefully enjoying inside the mother for the past nine months. What we are trying to do by using the 5 "S's" is to create a so-called "4th Trimester." The new trimester takes place in a different environment (the outside world), but the goal is to mimic the previous environment (the mother's womb) as much as possible.

- **Swaddling**: Snug swaddling with a wrapped and tucked blanket provides the continuous touching and similar support that your baby was experiencing within the womb. Remember, he was in some pretty tight quarters, especially towards the end. What you will likely see is that even now, tighter is preferred and more soothing to him. Being swaddled has a calming effect on most babies. In contrast, being able to freely move their own arms and legs often irritates them. A good swaddle also prevents them from waking or startling themselves from the spastic jerking thing that babies do, called the Moro reflex. A quick involuntary jerk can upset them and ruin a good nap. Swaddling with a baby blanket is a skill that you must master. I have heard of a few babies that didn't like to be swaddled, but they are in the minority. It was like cotton-wrapped Ambien™ to all four of my boys. Do some online searches, watch some videos, and ask the staff for help. There are a few techniques that you can use to get a good wrap. You'll be amazed at the Houdini acts they can pull off if they are swaddled with inferior technique. There are many swaddling blankets and wraps on the market that attempt to make it easier. Some of these may come in handy later, but for now, most of them are way too big for what you need. The standard, blue and pink striped hospital blanket will do just fine once you get the setup and the technique down.

- **Side/Stomach position**: The infant is placed on his side or stomach to provide a reassuring and comfortably familiar position. He is not left alone in this position. Typically, this is used when you are holding him. "But never use the stomach position for putting your baby to sleep," cautions Karp. Sudden Infant Death Syndrome (SIDS) is linked to stomach-down sleep positions. When a baby is in a stomach-down position, do not leave him, even for a brief moment. Learn how to hold him in a comfortable, stable, side position. Also, learn how to let him rest on your chest, on his stomach, while holding him when you are lying down, or rocking. A change of position can be just the thing he needs to relax and settle down.

- **Shushing sounds**: I'm not sure of the historical origins of the use of the "shhh" sound, but it's a universal noise that makes all people get more quiet. Maybe it's a conditioned and learned behavior, or maybe it's just a natural thing. In any case, it works on babies. Karp's theory is that these sounds imitate the continual whooshing sound made by the blood flowing through arteries near the womb. Babies have heard lots of fluids moving around for the last few months. Doing this in conjunction with some of the other "S's" can be a very powerful soothing tool. There are many noise-making products in the baby aisle. Some of them even have the heartbeat sound as one of the options. I don't think the heartbeat sound is necessary, nor do I recommend using a sleep machine for bedtime. I'll explain that in more detail soon enough. Just use your voice for the "shhh," and use it when you need a little extra something to calm him.

- **Swinging/Swaying**: Newborns are used to the swinging motions within their mother's womb, so entering the outside world with new gravitational properties is like a sailor adapting to land after nine months at sea. "It's disorienting and unnatural," says Karp. Rocking in a chair, car rides, and other swinging movements can all help and may be preferred. Again, there are many commercially available products to help gently keep your baby moving. If you get a swing, get one that swings both front to back and also has a side to side option. Some babies hate one motion and love the other. You never know until you try. If you buy one, get one that is the easiest to clean. If it has 34 fabric pieces and requires tools to disassemble before the pillow can be thrown in the washer, you may want to look for another option. More important than the swing is your ability to master the baby sway. Find a smooth, repeatable, gentle motion to soothe your baby while he's in your arms. It may take a few experimental variations before you find the right rhythm that he prefers.

- **Sucking**: "Sucking has its effects deep within the nervous system," notes Karp, "and triggers the calming reflex and releases natural chemicals within the brain." Babies are born with an ability to suck and a brain that instinctively seeks to do so. Whether it's a breast, a bottle, a pacifier, your finger, his finger, or your belt loop, he will root and latch onto most anything small enough that is within tactile range. My only advice here is not to force the pacifier. Use it when you need it, but don't assume that he needs it too often. We need to let our children learn how to self-soothe. Parents love quiet, and therefore love pacifiers. Having a pacifier in the mouth all day should not be the norm. Use it like you would use medication, that is, only when absolutely necessary. Many parents overuse pacifiers, and it can create numerous problems later. Dependency is one issue, speech delays and improper teeth development are others. I'm not saying that you should never use it. Just don't use it all the time, and have some criteria for when and how to use it. For a quick fix, try your pinky finger knuckle.

In addition to the genius advice by Dr. Karp, I have another hack that will add two more letters to add to the litany of "S's." One is "P", and the other is "V."

- **(P) Patting**: Softly patting a small child on the back while holding him is also quite soothing. You have seen parents do it thousands of times but thought nothing of it. You've seen it because it works. Swaying and patting together is pure magic. It can become a potent conditioning tool that immediately soothes a child and even induces sleep.

- **(V) Voice:** Your baby has hopefully heard your voice for months. I trust that he has heard it in a self-disciplined, pleasant tone as well. There is just something about a man's voice. If you are like me, you will notice that your child responds favorably to your masculine voice. Speak deeply, but softly to him. He will often stop whining instantly and will eventually open his eyes and turn his head toward the noise to see his favorite guy. Tone is very powerful, and your voice can cut right through chaos and bring immediate comfort. Try whispering too. If your volume is lower, the tiny, upset person will have to lower his volume just to be able to hear you.

It's a giant list, but now you have a complete S-S-S-S-S+P+V. I assure you that it's a proven winner, even if at times it seems like overkill. My secret combo weapon is a baby in a good swaddle, positioned on his side facing me (stomach to stomach), held close to my body, with a steady sway, patting him softly on the back with a light "shhh" as needed. It's kind of like rubbing your stomach while patting your head and making a cappuccino with your feet. You'll get it down in time. Perfecting this combo has made me look like a baby whisperer to many people. I especially love using it to help calm someone else's baby that they say is inconsolable. It works nearly every time. Honestly, in the rare event that it fails, it's probably because of colic or hunger.

These things take some practice and a little time. Take them on as a challenge, as essential skills that you must master. Passing the baby to his mom every time he cries is a failure. I repeat, a failure. I hate seeing guys do this. It's sadly a common practice for many males. If you can only hold him or care for him when he's happy, you aren't much help. You must be able to soothe him too. I dare to say that you need to be the best one at it. You will probably be sharing the time holding your new one with your wife, family, and friends. Put in the time whenever possible, and do the work. It won't be needed as much in the first few days but will be of tremendous value in the weeks and months to come.

Hit the Road, Jack

Finally, a discharge that everyone welcomes with a smile.

Leaving the hospital with the first child is a little strange. It feels like they shouldn't authorize you to just put him in your car and go home—at least not without taking classes, getting a permit, a confetti drop, and a police escort or something even more dramatic. A welcome home trip and reception like they had on American Idol™ would seem more appropriate.

Regardless, it's finally time to go home, which may come as a relief to you, knowing that real food and a comfortable bed are in your near future. On the other hand, it may be very intimidating and concerning. You don't know what you are doing yet, and this little being that you are responsible for is a big deal. Can you imagine any other job where the boss hires you with no experience, then explains that this will be the most challenging, most important, and most demanding thing you have ever done, and then asks you to start the job immediately?

If you think too much about it, it will inspire fear and anxiety. So just don't think too much about it. You will learn on the fly. There is no better education than experience, and you will get plenty of it along the way. I will get you started, and you will be in a better place than 90% of the rest of the new dads in the world. People that are much less prepared, with less intelligence and less will, do survive this. You will be fine.

Once Mom has recovered, and everyone has passed all of their inspections, the attending doctor will sign off on the official discharge orders. This frees your family to be released from the hospital's care and go home. On the first baby, most hospitals will keep you at least two nights, if not three or more. By baby number four with good rapport, you can get discharged faster than you can get food from a taco truck. It's totally a judgment call, and everything is negotiable. If you have some extra family help at home, and everyone is doing well, I say, get out of there as soon as possible. If you have full coverage insurance and want to have a few extra days to learn how to change, feed, and swaddle, and delay full responsibility and custody of this little family member, you may want to stay until they kick you out. An extended stay at an obnoxiously expensive, uncomfortable resort with bad food is never a request that my wife makes.

My wife always prefers to go home as soon as possible. One time, we were growing impatient and worried that another day would be added to our stay and our bill. I asked the nurse, "What happens if we just leave?" We had not been officially discharged yet, even though the last doctor verbally said that we were all clear. We were waiting for the next attending doctor that would make rounds several hours later. We were on the cusp of potentially having to stay another night if the doctor didn't come on time or if she didn't agree with the previous one. The nurse answered the question candidly and informed us that she could not restrain us or keep us there against our will. She also pointed out that it's not technically kidnapping if it's your child and your hospital bracelet barcodes match. Instead of bolting for the door, she told us that she would make a few calls and get the paperwork faxed over. We left legally and followed protocol, after all. I've been to Alcatraz and seen the TV specials on it. I'm confident that I could have contrived a plan to get out of that hospital if it came down to it.

Someone will likely come with a wheelchair to escort your rock star wife. In my experience, this person is usually the coolest employee in the entire establishment. I'm not sure why, but it's proven to be true time and again. Of all the duties at the hospital, I imagine that one is a pretty happy gig. I think it's customary for the new mom to hold the baby on the way out as she is wheeled to the door. Your job during the transfer will be mostly to look happy while other people in the hospital give "Oh, how sweet" looks. You carry the bags, making sure that you don't leave anything behind, and get the car ready. Don't forget to get some good pics of the departure too.

Before you bolt for the door, you'll need my discharge hack. This simple practice is quick and valuable: grab everything that you can legally take from the room. You'll need to leave the bed and the rock-hard chair, but get all of the unused disposables. Let your favorite nurse know that you are leaving soon and ask what you are allowed to take home and if there are more free samples or goodie bags. You likely paid for everything currently in the room, but there are always some freebies too. Many companies give the hospital lots of free stuff so that you get hooked on their products. Get diapers, wipes, soaps, lotions, and anything that they are willing to give you. Once, I left with a free car seat, a fully stocked diaper bag, and four cases of pre-mixed formula bottles. If you are bottle feeding at all, the most useful thing for you to get is the ready to drink, 2-ounce formula bottles.

Don't forget the plastic rings and nipples that go on them. These are disposable, one-time-use, ready-to-drink bottles. Those little suckers are not cheap. You can thank me later when the free ones run out and you're forced to buy the first case at the full retail price. As long as they are free, snag as many as they will allow. Our family graduates to glass bottles later, but for now, don't bust my chops on the plastic argument. If you are a save-the-planet minded, hater of plastic, you may want to make an exception for a month. I'm sure a few of our old bottles are floating next to your coffee K-cups in an ocean somewhere, but I'm OK with that. We do recycle everything if that makes you feel any better. Take conveniences when you can get them in the first stage of this journey. Trust me.

At this point, you've already installed the baby's seat in your car and learned how to use it. You did that already, right? The wheelchair pusher will escort your newly expanded family out. Now it's time to buckle this tiny, awesome person into his safe seat, which suddenly seems to be a gargantuan, over-padded throne. Everyone is set to go. It feels like there should be some formal send off procedure, official training course with final instructions, a field guide, and a contract to sign. There is nothing. The guy who rolled you out, who has had no infant training, simply closes the car door, says farewell, and returns to the facility to find another family to roll out.

Your only job now is to drive the family car home safely. You have been operating your vehicles unconsciously and haphazardly for many years. However, this time, you religiously abide by everything you learned in driver's ed. You suddenly transform into a very emotional, defensive driver and realize all the dangerous moves that other ignorant drivers make.

3 DAYS AD

Mama, We're Coming Home

Ahh, the sweet smell of home, your bed, your kitchen, and your mother-in-law.

Hopefully, everything is well cleaned, organized, and prepared for the new baby to come home. Cribs, bassinets, changing tables, and feeding stations are all in place. Supplies are stocked, and everything is a go.

It is so much better to come home to an organized, tidy home, rather than one that needs immediate attention. Everyone is tired, and there is much to do. Cleaning and organizing shouldn't be on the list now. You have no idea how the new routines will pan out, but you know that there is work to do and less time available than ever before. Please don't allow your wife to return to a messy abode. You may need to go home for a few hours the day before you are discharged from the hospital to tidy things up. Maybe you can call in a favor and get a family member to help, or even pay someone to do it while you are at the hospital. Just make sure that all the dishes are clean and put away, all the laundry is neatly finished, and every room is clean. Leave nothing undone, and grab some flowers while you're at it. This peaceful and organized home environment can help reduce the emotional stress level. Knowing that these things are already complete will ease everyone's mind, even if it is not noticed or mentioned.

Now we need to talk about what needs to be set up for a smooth transition home. Obviously, you need at least one place to change the baby. I recommend having two designated spots. These could be a table equipped with a changing pad or just a simple blanket on a bed for now. One changing station should be where he will sleep, and the other spot should be where everyone will be relaxing and recovering. Just be sure to have a waterproof, washable (or disposable) covering wherever the locations are. Little people will urinate with uncanny timing during a change. Less often, but also plausible, is an unexpected number two while you are in mid-change, reaching for some diaper cream. You need to have diapers, wipes, and clothing within reach so that you never take your hands off the baby. They don't roll over in the early days, but the practice of keeping a hand on them at all times should be ingrained in your mind forever and remain a mandatory staple for the changing process.

The idea of using a baby wipes warmer seems nice, but in reality, isn't all that practical or necessary. That is one of those 214 things that you register for because you think it sounds good at the time. You maybe even pondered how satisfying warm wipes would be on your own bottom. Regardless of your affinity for a warm, moist cleanse, it's just not a legitimate need. Babies will likely not like to be changed either way, warm or cold. Once you get good at it, it only takes a few seconds, so he won't be upset long. The problems with warmers are that they must remain plugged in, they require an extra step to load the wipes into it, and they can be incubators for mold. A warm, wet, dark location is perfect for bacteria to grow. Also, you will change your baby like 1,000 times a week. You will not always be in a place with a warmer nearby and won't have a battery operated one in your bag (although I'm sure they exist). Just let the little one get accustomed to a room temperature diaper change, and he will be okay. Hacking fatherhood is about simplifying and streamlining as many processes as possible.

If you are breastfeeding, you will want to have a nursing pillow for Mom, like a Boppy™. These are useful and help her support and position the baby during feeding. You may also need a breast pump. These are expensive, and a lot of mothers have one in the closet sitting idle. Ask around, and see if someone may have one that you can borrow before you purchase one. The more personal parts of the apparatus are either disposable or washable. They can easily be sterilized or replaced. The breast pump will allow the mother to pump excess milk and keep it for later use. That means you can help. I highly recommend you do the feeding as often as possible. The process of using a breast pump can be awkward, laborious, uncomfortable, and even embarrassing for women. It's not a spectator sport, and she may not want you to help in this process. Everyone is different, so like everything else, just talk to your spouse, and respect her preferences and needs.

Ask your pediatrician about storage times and methods for keeping breast milk safe for your baby's consumption. Most people keep it in the fridge for a few days. Some people freeze it and build up a supply for much later. It's good to have some back stock so that you can do some feeding with a bottle at times and so that you have a second option when breastfeeding is not ideal. You may have a busy day when a bottle works much easier. Also, there are some specific times when breastfeeding is not recommended. An example would be when the mother has to take certain medications that can be transmitted through the milk to the baby. Many vitamins, supplements, antibiotics, and other medicines can enter the breast milk. If your wife is taking any of these, be sure to ask your doctor about all of them.

Whether pumping or solely formula feeding, having many bottles on hand is crucial. You will need to sterilize the bottles, nipples, and rings by boiling them or using a high temp setting in the dishwasher before the first use. You probably want to do it after every use, not just the first time out of the pack. Discuss this with the doctor too. We use glass bottles instead of plastic because we boil ours regularly and don't want any potential plastic contaminants. They also last a lot longer and can be used for years to come with multiple children. The downside is that they are heavy and breakable. You decide what works best for your family.

If using formula, there is an easy hack for making rapid bottles and staying on track. I mentioned the 2-ounce, ready-to-feed bottles from the hospital. These are super convenient, and I recommend using them for at least the first few weeks. You especially want to keep them in the diaper bag for when you are away from home. They cost more, but they eliminate the need to carry water and formula that need to be mixed. Much larger bottles of pre-mixed formula are available at the pharmacy or grocery store. If you buy the larger bottles, be careful, they may have a short expiration window once you open them. Check the labels and plan accordingly. You don't want to waste the pre-mixed formula because it's pricey. When the little guy is only eating two ounces at every feeding, you may not finish the entire large bottle before it expires. They will also need to be refrigerated, which means you will have to add a warming step before feeding.

Get yourself a bottle drying rack, a bottle warmer, and a dishwasher basket for nipples and rings. If you don't have a dishwasher, you will need to designate a basket or storage container for the used and uncleaned parts. Have enough bottles, nipples, and rings for two to three full days of feeding. Always rinse them out immediately after feeding to remove all the visible residue, even if they aren't getting the final, high-temp wash yet. Only fully cleaned supplies go on the drying rack, ready to assemble after the final wash. I repeat, only clean ones go on the drying rack. When it's feeding time, put the correct volume of water or breast milk in a clean bottle. Heat it in the bottle warmer to the proper temperature. Test the water or milk to make sure it isn't too hot. If using formula and water, dump your correctly measured formula into the bottle, put on a new nipple and ring, and shake. If you use a bottle that is an ounce or two bigger than you need, you get a much better mix when shaking it. In other words, allow some room for mixing. If it's too full, you won't get a good mix, the formula will clump together, and you will need a small stirring spoon to finish the job.

After feeding and burping, rinse everything out and place the rinsed parts into the dishwasher basket or "dirty" container. Once per day, or every other day if you have enough supplies, you will run the dishwasher or hand clean and boil all the parts and reload them onto the rack. There will be a lot of bottles in the coming weeks, and having a simple, streamlined system will prove to be very beneficial. Good systems make life easier.

Don't expect your wife or mother-in-law to do this stuff; keeping the bottles clean and ready for use is an easy job and a way for you to be more useful. Make life as easy as possible for your new baby's mother, even if you are exhausted. Minimize her responsibilities, and keep doing the work.

Getting in the Groove

Do you think he's tired? He's probably just hungry. Maybe wet? It's probably colic.

If you have not been paying attention to anything in this book so far, wake up now. This chapter will elevate the happiness in your home and decrease the stress on the entire family. It will be tricky to get started, but if done well, will dramatically improve your success. Discipline in the beginning makes for predictability, structure, and confidence in the end. Investing time and attention now will build consistent patterns that pay major dividends. Humans are adaptable and will learn to function within most any system. If we strategically build that system, we can control many of the behaviors within it. You must create the master plan for the little guy to learn the preferred behaviors. Most people fail to build a deliberate plan, and not surprisingly, success is never achieved. Floundering all day with an unhappy, unrested, hungry child will certainly result in the absence of a structured plan. Some parents succeed in having a plan but deviate from it or abort the mission when it gets hard. They plan to fix it later, and just try to survive the day. The delay goes on for days, then months. Usually, the fix never happens, and if it does, the problem is much harder to reign in.

Having a structured routine must be deliberate, or the success will never materialize. This is the case for most every area of our lives, but certainly true for new families starting a new routine and a new way of life. Many people fly by the seat of their pants in everything in life. They are undisciplined and unorganized, which leads to a more stressful life. Luckily for my children and me, my wife has never been undisciplined or unorganized. She has taught me that these traits make parenting so much more successful and remarkably easier. We watch other parents maintain a level of confusion, frustration, unrest, stress, and unpredictability. These people are missing something of utmost importance: a regimented, automatic, unchangeable routine.

You must establish a routine now. It's a boring concept, but highly effective. A set schedule for feeding, wake times, napping, and bedtime is imperative. This is a huge parenting hack. Much like we discussed earlier with proper eating, training a child's tastes and dietary habits, we will again condition a child to act in a favorable, healthier pattern. You will be able to train your baby when to be tired and when to be hungry. Having a predictable eating and sleeping schedule means that Mom and Dad won't be losing their minds, confused and wondering why the little one is crying again. The steady routine will allow you the opportunity to have a fitness workout, go to church, go out to eat, have a phone conversation, or even have an uninterrupted bathroom break for yourself, without the world imploding and sending you into a hair-pulling rage. You can make appointments and schedule your life because you will know exactly when your baby will need what he needs. I cannot stress enough how important this is. We must craft and commit to a rigid schedule early, then adhere adamantly to the plan.

Feed at the same times every day. Don't make excuses or special provisions and wing it on the fly. If you do, they will happen almost every day, and your schedule will be a joke. If you have to stop the car on the road trip to be able to feed on time, do it. If you have to excuse yourself from the party early to get your baby in bed, do it. What you do now will determine what you will have to do later. Please read that last sentence one more time. People will not understand, and they will think you are paranoid and overbearing. I'm fine with that. Chaos is the norm for most parents, but not for you. You are extraordinary. You are a hacker. You are winning at the same game that is making everyone else miserable. Stick to the plan without outside pressure or exceptions. Cultivate your rigid feeding schedule based on the doctor's recommendations. If you need two ounces every three hours, that's the plan. Don't get one ounce in now and try to get the other ounce in 45 minutes later. Keep trying until the little guy takes the full recommended amount, or until you know, it cannot be done. If he doesn't finish the bottle, don't supplement 30 minutes later during a non-feeding time. Wait until the next time slot and try to get the full bottle in then. He will be hungrier, and you will have a better chance to get the full bottle finished.

Remember, you are training his system. If you allow an ounce here and an ounce there, and just feed when he seems hungry, he will learn that feeding routine and you will forever struggle to get him to eat a full meal. We must train his system when and how it will receive food. A good meal means that he isn't going to be hungry for a few hours. A partially consumed, poorly executed feeding results in a child that will be angry at any time (or the entire time) during the next few hours. Of course, some feeding times will take a while based on how fast he drinks and how well he burps. You will probably stop after every half ounce to burp him in the beginning. Your pediatrician will tell you when to change the schedule and the volume.

After feeding time comes wake time. Wake time is a fatherhood hack that you will come to cherish; it is a happy time for playing, speaking, and interacting. It's also part of the conditioning that will begin to be a reliable cue for nap time. Wake time should be stimulating and engaging for both baby and parent. It will take time for it to feel like your baby is being engaged or stimulated, but the routine starts now. You will both cherish the face time, and he will learn to stay awake and alert for it in time. He will also be learning your voice along the way. Eventually, there will be eye contact, smiles, and direct response. Even though it won't seem like much, stick with the plan. As Marcus Lemonis confidently says to owners as he is rebuilding their business, "You've got to trust the process." The baby will learn to be playfully awake and happy after each feeding. The goal is feed, wake, sleep, in that order. If it gets out of sequence, he will start falling asleep when he should be eating and will fail to finish a good meal. That will lead to him waking upset before he is fully rested because he's hungry. Eventually, he may depend on the bottle to fall asleep. It's an unhealthy cycle. Keep the proper sequence, and train him to do it your way. Eat well, then play well, then sleep well. This is good advice for humans at any age.

Wake time will vary in length based on how long it takes to feed. That's because next to feeding, the other important and strictly regimented time slot is for rest. Feeding has a set time, and resting has a set time. Whatever time is between these two is the wake time. If it takes a long time to eat and burp, wake time may be shorter that morning. Thirty minutes is probably a good expectation for wake time. Most people start to get a little sleepy about 30 minutes after a full belly. Babies are no exception.

After feeding and a stimulating wake time, it's time for a nap. Like feed times, the nap time is laid out on the schedule and religiously respected. Training a child when to nap is vital for your well-being, and for his. In time, you can plan the things that you need to get done every day around the time he will be sleeping. You might just want to take a nap yourself. With this system, unlike most parents who are just winging it and struggling to survive, you will have options. His growth and development depend on getting proper rest. He will sleep a lot in the first few weeks, and you will be grateful for it. Again, make out a schedule for feeding and sleeping, and follow it faithfully.

It's important for nap time it to be quiet and undisturbed. Don't come in and out of the room. Visual stimulation affects his resting state, so movement and visual activity in the room needs to cease. You may want to keep the door open so that you can hear. That's fine, just try not to go in and out until the nap is over. Naps are easier in the early days, but will only remain that way if you get the routine down now. I recommend not using a noise maker or sound machine. The reason I say this is because if a child becomes dependent on a particular noise to fall asleep, he will learn to require it forever. That could be problematic later if you do not have access to that same noise. Babies can become accustomed to the regular ambient sounds that are in a home, including daily things like urban noise, other children in the house, or noisy neighbors. That is a good thing and certainly recommended. Don't train him to require an environment that is impossible or difficult to recreate.

Just remember that whatever you do, stay consistent. Swaddle the same way every time. Rock the baby or sway with him the same amount of time every time. Sing, talk, or pray softly the same way every time. Dim the lights the same way every time. All of these things will be cues that he learns to associate with sleep time. Later, he will start to relax during the swaddle. He will yawn while you sway, and get heavy eyes while you sing. It's like Pavlovian magic.

I want to recommend a sleeping hack that has always worked well for us. During nap time, leave a small lamp or brighter nightlight on in the room. Maybe leave the blinds open a little. This bit of light is only used during daytime napping. That light should be extinguished or made substantially dimmer at night for his actual bedtime. This simple change serves two important purposes. One is that it will allow the baby to learn to differentiate between nap time and bedtime. We want bedtime to have a few extra cues so that the little guy will learn to sleep through the night. The other reason to keep a brighter light on during rest time is for him to learn to sleep and take naps in the daytime light. There will be times when you need him to rest in the stroller, in the car, or at a foreign locale that he isn't accustomed to. It will sometimes be impossible to make some places dark. You don't want full darkness to be the determining factor in whether he takes a good nap or not. Whatever they are trained to do early will be what they require later. Keep it simple, and plan ahead. Make the standard sleeping environment one that is easily reproduced. New babies naturally spend a lot of time sleeping in the beginning. The easy sleeping in the first few days means that setting up a schedule will be much easier now than it will be later. You may find that it's harder keeping him awake during wake time than it is keeping him asleep during rest time.

Now comes the hard part. You have to decide how long rest time will be, and make it a rigid part of the schedule. Every child needs a different amount of rest, so it may take a little while to figure out the best routine. Then you must have the discipline to allow the rest to happen. The child may not be sleeping the entire time, but he needs a designated amount of quiet, lower light, rest time. Try to stay out of there for the whole time if possible. This can be difficult when initially establishing the routine, and he cries as soon as you leave the room. There is an overwhelming urge to go in there and fix everything. The desire to check on him, pick him up, to grab a pacifier, or to rock him to sleep is insanely difficult to suppress, especially for your first baby. It's a real struggle because the sound of a crying baby instinctively bothers us and calls us to action. You want him to stop crying, for him and for everyone else. A baby's cry is stressful for everybody within hearing proximity, but even worse when that baby is your own. Just remember that you are establishing routines and patterns now, and the effort will produce favorable results later. If he observes that you will come in every time he cries for more than four minutes, he will learn to do just that and to expect it. You are also doing him a disservice if you don't allow him adequate time to get tired and to fall asleep. He must learn how to self-soothe and how to fall asleep without your constant intervention. His sleep patterns will suffer and so will his health if he cannot get proper rest. Some doctors say that crying is good exercise and that babies need it. I'm not saying to let him scream in agony for an hour. However, five to ten minutes may be just what he needs to tucker out and fall asleep on his own.

Recognize and appreciate the difference in when he is just tired and when you need to check on him. Babies have different tones, volumes, pitches, and breathing patterns that will let you know what they are thinking and feeling. In time, you will learn to differentiate between his cries. As long as everything is OK on the monitor, you will be able to give him a few extra minutes to settle down by himself. My advice is to give a child up to 15 minutes to stop crying and fall asleep on his own. (You should probably start with 10. Ask your doctor.) After 15 minutes, go in and soothe the unsettled baby if you need to. You will find that most of them will get tired (remember, crying is a form of exercise for them) and fall asleep in much less than fifteen minutes, and your services will not be necessary. You make the judgment call. Maybe you can start with ten minutes. Even that long can seem like an eternity for new parents. It's really hard, so be ready for it. Many times, he will fall asleep when you are on your way to the room to rescue him at the ten minute mark. Sometimes he just needs 20 more seconds.

When the feeding and resting schedule is established, it must be sacred. Everyone must respect and follow it. That includes babysitters, caregivers, and grandparents. Enforcing the schedule with them can be tough. Grandmothers may have their opinions and not like your schedule. Other caregivers may be careless and flippant about it. Do what you can to guard and preserve the schedule. It matters. When that child is six months old and finishes every bottle, plays happily, goes down for a nap without a single fuss, and sleeps for ten hours every night, you will realize that your hard work and diligence has provided sweet success.

Happy Nappy Time

**"I'll be right back, y'all, I'm just going to put the baby down."
Three minutes pass... "OK, I'm back." The couple that is over
for dinner is stunned, and the guest wife says, "That's it? The
baby is down? Dang! That must be nice." You give a confident
nod, saying nothing, but think to yourself, "Yep! It sure is."**

The bedtime routine is not all that different from nap time. There
are just a few other cues that will let your baby know that it's nighttime,
not just nap time. Soon enough, that means sleeping all night. That will
be a huge win when it's achieved. Hopefully, it won't take too long to
get there.

One powerful cue for babies to realize that it's almost bedtime is
a warm bath. After getting the last meal of the evening, it's time for
a bath. I am going to recommend that you do bath time every night
at the same time, instead of some random time during the day. Sure,
you will need a supplemental bath from time to time from a diaper
that exploded, a messy meal, or a spit-up bomb. I am talking about the
elective evening bath here, not an emergency cleanup. Let part of the
last wake time of the day be bath time. Just like the other conditioning
methods we have been discussing, you will see that after getting into
the groove with this routine, the bath will be a tool to calm and relax
the baby. He will start to get heavy eyes when he feels the warm water.

I recommend a baby bath that has a soft hammock type sling in
the center. They keep the baby from sliding on a hard, wet surface. The

cloth part is removable and washable. They are superior to the ones that have a permanent foam pad which tends to get moldy over time. Get one that has a reservoir under it that has enough room to scoop water out with a cup to gently pour on the baby. If it has a basin, you don't have to use the bathtub and do the uncomfortable bend over the side position. One that fits into the kitchen sink is very handy too. Just make sure that once the baby is big enough to reach the faucet handles, that they are out of reach. Otherwise, in a split second, he could move the handle and change the temperature to a dangerous level. Put the baby bath in the sink, shower, tub, on the floor, or wherever works for you. Always keep a hand on him, just like when changing clothes or diapers. Gather everything that you could possibly need beforehand because you absolutely, under no circumstances, may leave his side during a bath.

After the warm bath is complete and PJ's go on, follow with your usual pre-rest ritual with swaddles, sways, rocks, reads, or songs. This time, we need to make the room a little darker. If you have windows in the room, this will happen naturally, and he can distinguish between bedtime and naptime. Otherwise, you need to have a different, more dim nightlight for the evenings than the one you use during the day. For evenings, have just enough light so that you can come in to feed and change safely without needing to turn on anything else. The goal is to keep the environment the same, even during feeding or changing. For night feedings, you stay in the room for everything. Feed and change in the darker room and skip the standard wake time. In time, you will be able to change and feed without even waking him up.

I must now trudge into a topic that is sure to get me in trouble. Co-sleeping (bed sharing) with the baby is a habit that many parents get into, and I think it's a horrible practice. I am talking about allowing the baby to sleep with one or both of you in the same bed. Some parents do it out of fear and paranoia, some do it to make breastfeeding easier during the night, and some do it out of their desire to snuggle with their infant. I know many parents that have children ranging from 6 months to age 11 that can't get their child to sleep in their own bed alone. You want to talk about a strain on your rest, your peace of mind, and your love life? Allowing a temperamental baby to permanently sleep in your bed will wreak havoc on all three. To protect against this unending dependency of bed sharing, it's best just to forbid it from the get go. I have plenty of logical reasons to have boycotted it in my home. We have never allowed it, and everyone has been just fine. You may think I'm a monster, but hear me out.

The reasons to avoid co-sleeping are numerous and easy to understand. Here they are:

#1 - It's a safety issue. Having a small person sleeping next to one or two adults on a soft bed with fluffy pillows and blankets is dangerous. If someone rolls over, the baby can be injured, smothered, or pushed off the bed. Newborns are not supposed to have any blankets, bumpers, or pillows because they lack the strength and cognitive ability to move away from the item if it's covering their face and restricting breathing. Many people jerk, kick, or flinch during sleep. Your sweet little nugget of perfect DNA doesn't need to withstand a knee to the back of the head while you are dreaming of wrestling blue alligators with George

Bush on an airplane. A fall off the bed could be devastating as well. It's just risky and unnecessary. Sharing the bed with a new baby increases the incidence of SIDS (Sudden Infant Death Syndrome) by 5x in the first three months.

#2 - You are not getting good sleep. If the most valuable thing in the world, which also happens to be quite fragile, is sleeping next to you, you aren't ever totally relaxed. The people that defend their bed sharing habits will say that they always know where the baby is, can hear everything, and can respond to his needs immediately. They say this to defend the safety argument I made in point one, but in doing so, solidify my second point. They aren't sleeping well. You all need rest. We are all hyper-attentive in the beginning because it's daunting to think about caring for a helpless human all night long. Whether he is in the bed or not, this will be the case. Decrease the risk of something bad happening, and increase your chances of getting sleep.

#3 - You are creating dependency. As I have said numerous times, you must deliberately train your children. They are adaptable and will learn the systems if you consistently and diligently stick with the plan. He needs to learn to self-soothe and fall back asleep on his own. If he learns to depend on you to snuggle him every time he passes gas or whimpers, you both lose. There are plenty of things that he legitimately and desperately needs you to provide. There is no need to add more unnecessary things to that enormous list.

#4 - Your bedroom needs to be a sacred domain. You need a haven to escape to sometimes, and hey, one day you may want to practice the art of making babies again. Let's face it, you and the Mrs. desire and need to maintain a healthy, intimate relationship. If your three-year-old is in your bed for 10 hours a night, it tends to mess up the plan. Putting a child to bed, in his room, two hours before you plan to hit the hay can provide for some awesome opportunities. Having time for foreplay is good. I recommend "fiveplay" or "sixplay" whenever possible. Give yourselves the time, freedom, and opportunity to enjoy yourselves. Your marriage needs this. After returning home with a newborn, there will certainly be a necessary sexual hiatus to allow for mom's complete healing. Her doctor will let her know when normal sexual activity can be resumed. We do not, by any means, want the lack of that healthy activity to be prolonged or to become a permanent change because of a resident trespasser in the room.

#5 - The wedge effect. Many couples who allow co-sleeping end up sleeping in separate beds. The child prefers one or the other parent, who obliges the child's incessant need to be in their bed. As the child gets older and bigger (or as the parents get older and bigger), one parent decides to take one for the team, and they start sleeping separately. Sleeping separately isn't helping the marriage. Every parent needs a break from their kids and relaxing time to talk and be together. Don't let the thing that should function as marriage glue be the thing that separates you.

So, where should the newest member of the family sleep? I never said that he couldn't be in the room, just not in the same bed. The first week or two, let him sleep in a bassinet or crib in the same room just a few feet away. The goal and expectation need to be to move him to another room within the month. Some people purchase a "co-sleeper" bed that is a sort of three-walled bassinet that fits right up against your big bed, open side facing you, so you can reach in and out if the baby needs you without getting out of bed. If you like that, then fine. I think it's better to have a full bassinet or crib a little further away. If you need to change a diaper or feed the little guy, you have to get up anyway. No one will be hitting deep REM sleep for a while. You will get up to look, listen, and feel many times. You will relax more and more as time goes on, and that's a good thing because you would certainly crash if not.

The Hunt for the Missing Z's

It's still hard to fully comprehend that there is a tiny version of you now living in the house. It doesn't seem real, but you know it's not a dream because you haven't slept in days.

You will quickly find out that Mom and Dad are both totally drained. Like, the most sleep-deprived you have ever been in your life, insanely tired. The difference between now and those long and late nights before a child is that before, you had a chance to recover. The problem now is that the new gig never stops. You can't both sleep until noon tomorrow. So, what the heck are you supposed to do?

I have a hack for the common problem of early parental exhaustion. Most couples spend the first few nights together with the baby in the room, which helps you both learn and get comfortable with the new routine. It also means that you are both feeding and changing through the night, and both of you will be totally out of gas. No one gets any quality sleep. Constantly being interrupted all night long and expecting to perform well the next day is not sustainable.

You can survive doing this for a week or so, but a new plan will be a necessity of growing importance. You will need to take turns with the baby duties and take turns getting better rest. If you don't have an additional bed, cot, or sleeping bag in another room large enough for an adult human, you should probably make some arrangements to find one. If there isn't another bedroom, use the kitchen or the hallway. With the baby and one parent in one room, and the other parent having a temporary escape option, you both alternate turns enjoying better rest for longer periods of time. Instead of taking turns every three hours during the night and everyone waking every time in the same room, try separate rooms for longer, better rest. This is not a permanent plan and might not be necessary every night, but when you know you need it, use it. One of you takes the shift all night in the room with the baby, while the other parent sleeps all night in a room alone. If it's a bad night, and you just can't make it through, you can tap out and switch places. At least the other person had some quality rest. Breastfeeding can complicate this or render it impossible in some cases. If you have breast milk pumped or use formula, you will probably both love the idea of taking full night shifts. The benefit summary for this hack is simple. My wife and I luckily discovered it long ago. That is that one block of quality sleep plus one block of poor sleep is exponentially better than two blocks of inadequate sleep. Trading shifts gives you some time to recover so that you can perform at a higher level, instead of maintaining a compromised state forever.

Sleeping separately is temporary. Remember, I want you in bed with your spouse as much as possible, as soon as possible. As the feeding and sleeping schedule improves, you will get more and more time back with your spouse. The baby will begin to wake every six hours instead of every three. At that point, which will take several weeks, try to transition to him sleeping in another room, and use the baby monitor. Leave both bedroom doors open if it makes you feel better. When he starts sleeping eight hours, you will be elated and energized. Ten hours will be surreal and will make you feel like you are getting away with something. Until then, you may discover the value of power napping. Seize every opportunity to nap that comes along. Most grandmothers will gladly watch the baby for an hour or two while you both can rest.

1 WEEK AD

Beating the System and Saving Your Wallet

Hooray! There is a baby at home, and everyone is happy. You don't want to be a buzzkill, but waiting for the bills to come is building major anxiety. How does the rest of the world do this? This is going to cost a TON of money.

NOTICE: DO NOT pay any medical bills (in any category, for any family member) until you read this chapter.

If you have doubted the value of this book and your time investment up to this point, you can set your mind at ease. This chapter alone is worth thousands of dollars. I am certain that the following few paragraphs will produce a 100x return on your investment of purchasing this book.

Many times in life, we look around us and wonder how the rest of the world does it. What's the catch? What are we missing? When I got my first set of bills for maternity services and childbirth, I wondered just that. We had catastrophic health coverage insurance but no maternity coverage. As a self-employed person trying to get a career started, with no company policy, I had to scratch my head and wonder how people like me could afford to pay the $3,500 OB tab, the $1,500 for lab services, and the $6,000 in hospital fees. I was making a good living and making responsible fiscal decisions, but come on, how many people your age have $11,000 in cash lying around?

The answer to the, "How do people afford it?" question is simple. They usually don't! It's all a big, nasty game. Many people get their debt pardoned in full, some get sizeable discounts, others work out a feasible long-term plan to pay it off, and only a select few can write a check and pay for it.

Here's how it all works. Medical offices, labs, hospitals, and collection agencies all play an involved poker game with your healthcare and billing. Please forgive me for making generalizations and lumping all healthcare together, but for the most part, it's accurate and fair to do so at this point. Let's say that Bob needs a diagnostic procedure. The doctors' office needs to charge $100 for this procedure. Bob's insurance says that it covers 50% of this procedure. So, in order for the office to collect the $100 that they need to cover overhead and make a profit, they raise the fee to $200 and send the claim to the insurance company, who hopefully pays 50% of it. If Bob says that he has no insurance, they would just charge him $100 directly. If he has insurance, they set the fee higher and get the insurance company to pay a portion of it. The uncovered balance at the end is what is in question. In this case, it's the $100 not covered on the $200 bill. The office has a decision to make: Option A - Charge Bob the leftover $100? Option B - Offer him a discount on the remaining balance? Option C - Write the whole thing off and zero Bob's balance?

In Option A, after paying the deductible, a $40 copay, and filing insurance, Bob would have been better off having no insurance (or withholding the information that he is covered) and just paying $100 cash. Option B is common, but every office has a different method for determining what's left. Option C happens the most often, but you may not be the recipient of such handouts. Our example was for $100, but as you know, we are missing a few zeroes if we are talking about hospital and specialized services.

Our first child came when I was a grad student. At the time, we had a great insurance plan through my wife's workplace. Awesome! I never even received a final bill. We payed a few copays, and everything else was covered by the premium policy. When we had our second child, I was making a nice income and my wife no longer had the work policy because she was staying home. I had a high-deductible medical insurance plan, but to my unfortunate surprise, and contrary to what the agent said when she sold me that policy, I did not have maternity coverage on the plan. Everything was fairly routine for prenatal, delivery, and postnatal care for baby number two. I received the bills after everything was completed, and I owed about $9,000. Then, I did the most idiotic thing in the world. I actually PAID the bills—IN FULL. I thought that was what responsible, honest people did. I was grateful for a healthy child, and I had, in fact, saved the money ahead of time for the procedure. I was proud that I could pay for it, and my wife was impressed too. That "honest" and "responsible" decision cost me about $4,000. I'll explain. Just know this: you should NEVER pay the balance on the bill without negotiating. You should also NEVER agree to a payment plan based on their terms. Let me be clear, I am not saying that you should skirt any bills that you owe. I think you should absolutely pay for everything that you owe. You should just reduce that amount as much as possible, and do it on terms that won't jeopardize the financial security of your family.

Knowledge is power, right? Well, here is some knowledge, and therefore some empowerment for your situation: Most offices and hospitals expect to collect the insurance or entitlement program fees, and little to nothing more. They will attempt to collect as much as possible, but expect not to get much. That means that EVERYTHING is negotiable.

Here's what I know now, and what I have done over and over since my mistake. These finance hacks have saved me tens of thousands of dollars. Again, this is not just for childbirth. This applies to all healthcare. Here are some valuable things to consider:

#1 - Get an itemized bill. Ask the hospital, the labs, the anesthesiologist, and the doctors for a detailed, itemized bill for all professional services offered to you and your child. Nearly every time the list is inspected, you will find expensive items on it that are inaccurate. It may be $55 for a sanitary napkin package that was never opened, $178 for a disposable bedpan that was never used, or $1,244 for an infusion pump that you have never seen. Ask someone questions about the items that are unclear. Get all charges removed that aren't legit.

#2 - CASH is KING. The first strategy is to ask for the costs before they happen. Even if you have insurance, ask for the cash fees. Then ask how much those "reduced" cash fees are REDUCED even further if you pay them in full. Most offices offer a discount for paying in full. This could be a 5% to 40% discount. I find that it's typically around 20%. Remember, it costs the facilities a lot of money to administer payment plans, to chase and collect money, and to file legal collection services. Offices would much rather receive a certain amount, even if it's less, than chase uncertain money for an uncertain amount of time. Dishonest and desperate people are really good at disappearing, and the medical offices know this. Many organizations will not give you the discounted numbers if they know that you have insurance. Don't give them the card until you get the information you need. Once you have accurate fees based on having no insurance, then you provide your card and ask for the fees, coverage, and leftover amount if you were to go that route. Then ask how much that balance is reduced if you pay it in full. Now you have two options to consider for whether you even use your insurance or not. Don't be surprised when these two final balance numbers are thousands of dollars apart. Sometimes the insurance route is better, but I find that usually the cash option is best.

#3 - LIFE is UNFAIR, and the medical industry is too. Medical offices expect different amounts from different demographics. You can say that this is crooked and unfair or that it's charitable and kind. Your opinion on which side to take will likely depend on one variable: which side you are on. You can make up your mind on where you stand on these issues politically. I mention it just to paint the picture and remind you that there is no such thing as a free lunch. Someone is paying for it. Medical facilities accept state plans and accept fees much lower than standard as payments for services rendered. People who pay their own medical bills are charged much more because those few have to make up the difference. The hard truth is that your hospital payment has to be high to pay for the four behind you that will pay little or nothing.

Most hospitals accept entitlement plans and state sponsored discounted insurance and do not charge the leftover amounts back to the patient. It's often illegal to charge these patients the remainder of the unpaid portion because the medical practices have contracted to provide the services at the lower rate. However, if you don't have one of these plans, they don't always expect you to pay for the entire final balance either. Again, it may seem charitable or crooked, but the truth is that the facility has different expectations for different income levels. If you just write the check, as I did on baby number two, they will gladly accept it and never mention any of their relief programs or discount policies. ALWAYS ask if there is an income-based assistance, discount, or relief program. If you are a high-income earner, you may not qualify, but you must ask to know for sure. These in-house programs typically have a scale based on household income and the number of family members in that household. If you have more dependents and less income, you qualify for a larger discount. Just ask before you pay. You may be surprised at what is available to you. I did not qualify for any discounts on my last three children based on income and household size. That meant that my bill was much higher, but still negotiable. I'll explain later. Just know that this is yet one more level of possible discount before you get to that final bill.

#4 - Do not sign the first payment plan that they put in front of you. Debt can ruin your life. If you fall behind on paying your bills, default on a loan, go bankrupt, or foreclose on a home, it will affect you forever. In these catastrophes, your reputation, your credit rating, and your trustworthiness are damaged. It may cripple you and take a long time to recover from the devastation. A payment plan is a legal agreement in which, if you default, can cascade into major problems. If you sign it and fall behind, they can send you to collections, garnish your wages, or worse. Do NOT sign a plan that requires more per month than you are able pay.

What are you supposed to do? You let them know that you are doing the best that you can and that you will pay as much as you can per month. They may try to intimidate you, scare you, or strong-arm you into signing a payment plan. You do owe them money, but the amount and the schedule have not been legally assigned yet. If you are making payments every month, even if they aren't much, you will not likely be harassed. They just need to know that you are actively and consistently paying. If you cease making a monthly payment or two, then you will certainly start getting letters and phone calls. If you don't have an extra $400 per month, don't agree to pay that for the next 24 months. Assure them that you will pay them everything that you owe but that it will take some time. Tell them that you will send as much as you can every month, and do it. One reason to approach paying the bills in such a reserved way is to protect your family moving forward. But another reason to pay it slowly is that they will probably offer you a much better deal in a few months. It's crazy, but true. Many organizations will offer you a settlement to close out the account after a few months of bills trickling in. They will cut the bill by 10% to 50% if you agree to a payment plan, or give a more substantial discount to pay it in full. If you do sign a payment plan, I suggest a simple rule. This strategy applies for car financing and home mortgages too: only agree to a plan that you can easily afford to pay in half the time. In other words, get a monthly payment that is half of what you know that you can afford to pay each month, and plan on paying double each month to speed it up. That way, if there is any hardship or financial change, you know you can pay less and not get in trouble.

#5 - Kindness makes a difference. Appeal to whomever you talk to in the billing office, as a kind and compassionate person. You will want to cuss, call names, and burn the place down on numerous occasions, but you must resist, and keep your cool. Be patient and kind. Stand your ground, but don't be a jerk. They get two reactions in the office from people like you with an outstanding balance: One is bitter rage, and the other is a pity party followed by a sob story. Don't give them either of these, and you will be noticed and treated differently.

Talk to the same person every time, and build rapport with her. If she is out to lunch or out of the office, leave a message, and get back in touch when she returns. Do not work with another employee every time you call. Sticking with the same person will allow you to build the relationship and create personal accountability. There is still a human element to this process, and having a friend in the front office will prove to be very beneficial.

#6 - If you use the right language and delivery, it works. I want to give you a few lines to use that are proven effective when negotiating. But first, please know that most of these people are paid on a commission basis. Yep! They get bonuses for how much they collect and how much they successfully secure into a payment plan contract. This means that working out a deal with you to get something, is much better than getting nothing. If they think the full amount is out of reach, they will work to get you a deal because they want a piece of the pie. Simple human nature comes into play when dealing with collections officers.

These are the quotes that you need to have in your bag of tricks. Use with your discretion based on where you are in the process.

"How does this really work? How do regular people do this?"

"I tried to save money ahead of time, but I had no idea it would be this expensive."

"Does this eventually cause people to go bankrupt if they can't pay it?"

"I am so grateful for my child being here, and I want to pay what I owe, but this is going to take a long time to pay for."

"I don't know if we can afford this right now."

"If I only have 'x' amount of dollars for this, what are we going to do?"

"Someone told me that you give huge discounts if you pay in full. How much is the discount?"

"If I could borrow the money from a family member or my bank, or put it on a credit card, what is the discount for closing out the account in full?"

"I have a friend that got a 50% discount for closing his account. What is that program called?" (It's not a lie, I am your friend, right?)

These lines help communicate that you are responsibly concerned, but not a crook or a beggar. I have used these tactics with amazing results, saving my family (and others) tens of thousands of dollars. Do not let them know that you have an HSA account or how much money you have saved. They will want to know how much you can pay today. Negotiate, and then leave the discussion in a time of silence for a few weeks if needed. Allow them to provide a creative solution that works for you. Don't take the first offer. Let them think that you are going to pay $40 per month for eternity instead of agreeing to pay the $450 per month that they recommend. The deal will likely get better with time, especially if you play your cards well.

The last thing that you must do after you agree on a settlement amount is very important: verify that all charges have finished in the billing cycle and that nothing else will be added later. Ask for a formal letter stating that once the specified amount is paid, you, your baby, and his mother are cleared from all services up to the date of the letter. Get it in writing. After you pay, you may get a few late bills that have been "in processing" for some time and show up weeks later. Do not pay these late bills that come after your agreed date. Your letter states that these are not your responsibility. Your agreement closed all your accounts for all services rendered up until that point. You certainly should not pay for anything else later because of their billing and filing inefficiency. This is an all-inclusive, one-time deal. Once it's paid and you have a letter saying that your debts are satisfied, don't write another check.

A Father's Perspective

If men were solely responsible for carrying a child for nine months and delivering a baby, the human race would be extinct.

Stop for a minute, and think about the last nine months. Your special lady lying in the other room, attached to a pneumatic breast pump, sitting in a diaper full of ice has been through war. The magnitude of the hormonal changes, the surrender of personal privacy, bodily mutations and mutilations, pain, exhaustion, emotions, fear, and confusion have been an insanely grueling process. You and I could have never done it, much less done it that gracefully. Women were built for this and men most certainly were not. Her role is something in which you should marvel. Your role, my friend, is just beginning. Your role is of vital significance, though it doesn't have the same public spotlight or the fanfare.

Over the next few days, months, and even decades, be appreciative of your wife and her contributions. You need her for many roles that you simply cannot carry out on your own. You need her, and so does your precious new child (and future children). Be grateful that she is here. Praise her. Encourage her. Support her. Show little signs of appreciation. Do it verbally with compliments, and non-verbally with gifts and thoughtful gestures. Leave her notes, treats, and flowers. Make her coffee, prepare her dinner, and tuck her in at night. You know what she appreciates; do those things. Hopefully, you will want to do these things and will get satisfaction from showing your wife how appreciative you are of her. Reaffirm your love for her as often as possible. All of these little things matter and will continue to matter even more as life moves on. If you aren't a thoughtful person, set reminders on your phone, or put it on your calendar.

I know you're tired now and have a lot on your plate, but now is when you start showing her what you are made of. I know that there is a heavy load on your back and a lot of pressure, but now is when you reassure her that you aren't just acting like someone else, you are becoming someone else. Blow her mind, and show her a true man. Your heart can grow. Your endurance can grow. Your sense of self-worth can grow. Your abilities can grow. Your success can grow. If you give it all that you have and apply the lessons learned in this book, you will grow as a man, as a father, and as a husband. Remember, only thing that you can control in life is your effort. Be sure that your wife and child always know that you are maximizing that. You are a new person. You are a father. Your priorities have changed. Your heart will follow your head after you ingrain new habits and practices. Repetition is key. Stay the course. Do the hard work.

You and your wife now have a newly joined role. You are parents. You are a team and have been tasked with the most important of vocations. You will be battered and tested. You will lean on her strength at times, and at other times, she will lean on yours. Build your relationship now to grow the team resilience that you will certainly need later. Your spouse and your child come first, forever. Your comfort and happiness are no longer the top priority.

Don't just do fatherly things. Be a father. Be a man of character. A large portion of being a good father to your child means being a wonderful husband to your wife. Place both of their needs ahead of your own, and know that it's going to try you to your limits. I am convinced that most people give up when they are at about 40% capacity. Your body will tell you to quit way before you should. There is always more gas in the tank than the gauge reads. We are all capable of more than we think. Push through that limit with an intense will. Quitting is not an option. Take divorce off the table now, and eliminate it as a plan B. It's not the easy way out. Fight for your marriage. Remain faithful to each other, and make a commitment to work on the relationship continuously, whether you think it needs work or not. Communicate with each other, and don't let little things go on undone. Never go to bed angry. Talk things out, and constantly work on your love for each other. It is a process that requires constant, intentional attention. Schedule date nights, vacations, and time to play together. Everyone needs counseling, and everyone needs grace. Find mentors and professionals that can help. Plan ahead, and prevent problems. Build the foundation that can withstand the impending storm. It will come, and it may return more than once.

Saying that we are committed to a fruitful and harmonious relationship is easy, but cheap. Agreeing with my advice may be no problem for you. It's another thing entirely to pull it off and maintain a strong family through difficult times. Most every man intends to be a good dad and a good husband. He, at minimum, doesn't desire to be terrible at the jobs. As Mike Tyson said, "Every man has a plan until he gets punched in the face." So, what happens to all of the men with good intentions? They get tired. They get caught off guard and get disoriented because they weren't ready for what was coming. Getting knocked off your feet is natural and should be expected if you don't have a game plan and haven't prepared properly. Men get bored. They get needy. They get greedy. They place themselves first and think that they are entitled to a "better life." The grass is not greener on the other side. The world is lying to you about that. We must do the work. It will always be challenging, and it will take everything that we have to succeed.

The secret is profoundly simple: you have to believe that this child is more important than your own life and happiness. Your family deserves all of your love. Your sacrifice is worth it. They cannot thrive as well without you. You must believe that the marriage is worth fighting for because stable parents are worth so much to the children.

The amazing thing about love is that when you are willing to give up your happiness and faithfully make sacrifices for others, that's when you start to be truly happy. Please hear me clearly. The only way for you to be happy in life is to do this job well. That is, to be the best version of yourself and keep working to be better. Be the man that you were designed to be. You know that you are not average. If you love with everything that you have, you will be satisfied. Regret and guilt will swallow you if you don't leave it all on the field. I think I've said enough. The rest is up to you. Go do your thing, Dad.

Author Bio

Dr. Nate Dallas is a devoted husband of fifteen years and an energetic father to four boys. He is a dentist, a serial entrepreneur, and a lifelong learner. He has helped many people build products and businesses over the years, but his true passion is helping men grow and transform into the strong leaders that they were designed to be.

That's a Wrap

Whether you like it or not, that's it for now.

We have taken a tedious journey together. I'm proud of you. You've made it quite a long way in a short amount of time. I know that you don't prefer to be left here without a coach. Hopefully, I will have the next steps laid out for you in yet another book. Writing this has been a labor of love and a sizable challenge for me. I hope to be with you again in a second volume if that privilege is granted to me.

If this has been helpful to you, please leave a review on Amazon, or drop me a quick note on the website. Consider recommending it to a friend or giving it as a gift. If you hated it, it would be really great if you never mentioned it. Thanks.

Connect with the author or sign up for occassional updates at:
www.hackingfatherhoodbook.com